PROSPERO'S
KITCHEN

PROSPERO'S KITCHEN

Mediterranean Cooking of the Ionian Islands
from Corfu to Kythera

DIANA FARR LOUIS
& JUNE MARINOS

Illustrated by
JUDITH ANN LAWRENCE

M. Evans and Company, Inc.

New York

M. Evans and Company, Inc.
216 East 49th Street
New York, New York 10017

Library of Congress Cataloging-in Publication Data
Louis, Diana Farr, 1940–
    Prospero's kitchen : Mediterranean cooking of the Ionian Islands
from Corfu to Kythera / Diana Farr Louis and June Marinos ;
illustrated by Judith Ann Lawrence
        p.   cm.
    Includes bibliographical references and index.
    ISBN 0-87131-782-6 : $21.95
    1. Cookery, Mediterranean. 2. Cookery, Greek. 3. Ionian Islands
(Greece)—History. 4. Ionian Islands (Greece)—Social life and
customs.   I. Marinos, June. II. Title.
TX725.M35L68   1995
641.591822—dc20   94-49418
                                                                CIP

Design by Dirk Kaufman

Manufactured in the United States of America

9 8 7 6 5 4 3 2 1

CONTENTS

Introduction 7

◆

THE ROOTS °F IONIAN CUISINE 9

A Short History of the Ionian Islands *11*
Daily Life on the Islands *29*

◆

PREPARING THE KITCHEN 57

Prospero's Larder: Notes on the Ingredients *59*
The Olive Tree, Its Oil and Fruit *67*
The Wines of the Ionian *75*
Basic Recipes *81*

◆

THE BEST °F ISLAND COOKING 85

Appetizers, Soups, and Salads *87*
Cheese, Eggs, and Pasta *111*
Fish *117*
Chicken and Other Birds *131*
Meat *143*
Meat and Vegetable Pies *163*
Vegetable Dishes *175*
Breads *195*
Coffee and Desserts *205*
Cookies, Candies, and Preserves *227*

◆

Acknowledgments 239
Bibliography 241
Index 243

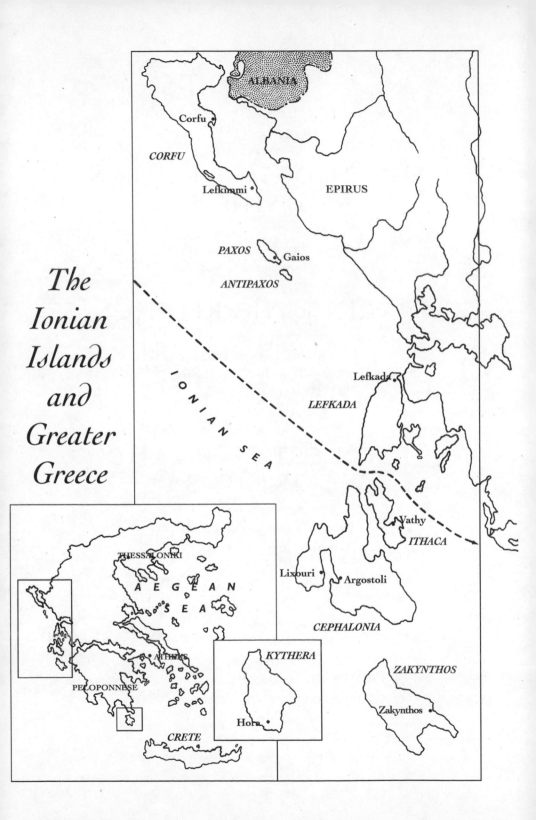

The Ionian Islands and Greater Greece

ALBANIA

Corfu

CORFU

EPIRUS

Lefkimmi

PAXOS
Gaios

ANTIPAXOS

I O N I A N   S E A

Lefkada

LEFKADA

Vathy

ITHACA

Lixouri
Argostoli

CEPHALONIA

THESSALONIKI

A E G E A N   S E A

ATHENS

KYTHERA

ZAKYNTHOS

PELOPONNESE

Zakynthos

Hora

CRETE

INTR°DUCTION

This book is about the cuisine of seven Greek islands—Corfu
(Kerkyra), Paxos, Lefkada, Ithaca, Cephalonia, Zakynthos, and
Kythera. The Greeks call them the Eptánisa or Seven Islands; the rest
of the world knows them as the Ionians, which is perhaps more accurate
for there are many more than seven if we count all of the smaller ones.
Many readers may only have heard of Corfu and Ithaca—the birth-
place of Homer's wily Odysseus—and might wonder why the cooking
of the Ionians should be different from that of the rest of the country.

Set in the Ionian Sea between Greece and Italy, these islands
were under western rule for eight centuries. Italians, mainly the
Venetians, influenced their architecture, art, language, music, society,
and culinary traditions; the French under Napoleon made a brief but
intense impact on their political consciousness if not their eating
habits; and the British governed them for fifty years, building roads
and schools, though, fortunately, having little effect on their love of
garlic and distaste for hard liquor.

When the foreigners finally departed, they left a legacy among
the upper and middle classes of western tastes and mannerisms,

superimposed on a foundation of rural traditions that had altered little in a thousand years. The resulting Ionian society was thus a fabulous hybrid, a flower grafted on indisputably Greek stock that possessed frills and variations unknown on the Ottoman-occupied mainland. It flourished especially on Corfu and Zakynthos—the most sophisticated and urbanized of the seven islands—and in the towns of Cephalonia, the largest of the group. But even the smaller, poorer islands have their Venetian castles and British residences, their recipes for English pudding or Venetian pastitsio alongside dishes that are characteristically Ionian.

Ionian cooking is quintessentially Mediterranean: laced with sweet virgin olive oil balanced by the acidity of tomatoes and lemon juice, heady with garlic, and reliant on herbs rather than piquant spices for taste. Even the party dishes have these simple, strong accents. Here you'll find imaginative ideas for vegetables—the "poor people's food" so rich in vitamins and low in cholesterol—and several one-dish meals from the time when cooks put all the ingredients in a single pot or in a portable oven and left it on the coals to simmer all day. Some of the recipes have Italian names or overtones, some are unequivocally native to Greece, some are refined urban dishes, some the simplest country fare. But above all, these are recipes for good things to eat, things that have made people happy and satisfied for generations.

We preface these recipes with a short introduction to Ionian history, and a tour of Ionian society in the nineteenth and first half of the twentieth century. Stories told by locals and foreign visitors help create a portrait of the special Ionian way of life that is rapidly vanishing in our homogenized modern world.

Prospero's Kitchen is dedicated to the delightful and hospitable people of all these islands and the magical memory of their bygone days and ways, evoked so beguilingly by Lawrence Durrell in his classic book, *Prospero's Cell*. If, as he and his cronies liked to imagine, Corfu really was the island of Shakespeare's sorceror, these are the dishes his spirits would have cooked.

THE ROOTS °F
IONIAN CUISINE

Odysseus routing the suitors, vase painting

To the left and right, outside, he saw an orchard
closed by a pale—four spacious acres planted
with trees in bloom or weighted down for picking:
pear trees, pomegranates, brilliant apples,
luscious figs, and olives ripe and dark.
Fruit never failed upon these trees: winter
and summer time they bore, for through the year
the breathing west wind ripened all in turn—
so one pear came to prime, and then another,
and so with apples, figs, and the vine's fruit
empurpled in the royal vineyard there.
Currants were dried at one end, on a platform
bare to the sun, beyond the vintage arbors
and vats the vintners trod; while near at hand
were new grapes barely formed as the green bloom fell,
or half-ripe clusters, faintly coloring.
After the vines came rows of vegetables
of all the kinds that flourish in every season,
and through the garden plots and orchard ran
channels from one clear fountain, while another
gushed through a pipe under the courtyard entrance
to serve the house and all who came for water.

Homer, *The Odyssey*, VII, ll. 113-134

A SHORT HISTORY OF THE IONIAN ISLANDS

If you look at a map of Greece, the Ionian Islands are tiny; on a map of the Mediterranean they are infinitesimal. And yet, from Corfu to Kythera, these islands—emerald baubles in the wine-dark sea between Greece and Italy—have been tickling the imaginations of poets and would-be conquerors for millennia. While Aphrodite was sometimes said to have been born from the sea foam off Kythera, the other islands conjure up images from Homer, for they belonged to Odysseus's kingdom.

It was on the shores of Corfu that Odysseus washed up after ten years of wandering the Mediterranean once the siege of Troy had ended. Homer's idyllic description of the gardens of King Alcinoos, who welcomed the bedraggled castaway into his palace and listened to his fantastic tales, makes the island sound like the Garden of Eden.

Over the centuries, many of the travelers who have visited Corfu were struck by its uncanny resemblance to the fabled land of the Phaeacians evoked by Homer. It seemed so green, so luxuriant. To this day fruits, grapes, and olives continue to flourish, and winter is a season of blossoms rather than snow. But location even more than fertility determined the fate of all the islands: they straddle the ancient trade routes between Italy and the Levant; they provided a gateway to the ports where the caravans from rich markets of the Orient, Asia Minor, and Egypt unloaded their treasures. Corfu, especially, was the key to control of the eastern Mediterranean until the mid-nineteenth century—when steam replaced sail and the Suez Canal was opened. It is no wonder that in the struggle to dominate this area; every power from the Romans to the French tried to occupy the islands. And would the British, who held them for fifty years after Waterloo, have been so willing to give them up if they had not had an empire on which the sun never set?

FROM CORINTHIAN COLONY TO ROMAN RESORT

Corfu leaves the realm of legend and enters history in 733 B.C., the date it was made a colony of Corinth, a trading power. The colonists named the island Corcyra, after a water nymph whom Poseidon abducted from her father, Oceanus, and whisked off to an island. Like so many merchants afterward, the Corinthians found Corfu to be an ideal way station for trade with Italy. The busy Corinthians also colonized Lefkas (Lefkada) a century later, digging the first channel through the narrow, shallow lagoon that separates it from the mainland. In the meantime, four strong city-states were growing on Cephalonia, and seafarers from Zakynthos were establishing trading posts in Crete, Italy, and as far away as Spain.

Before long, Corcyra was strong and prosperous enough to win its independence from Corinth and set up its own colonies, too. By the time of the Persian Wars (early fifth century B.C.), which it discreetly stayed out of, its fleet was second only to that of Athens. But friction persisted between Corinth and Corcyra, inflammatory enough, so Thucydides tells us, to upset the balance of power between Athens and Sparta and explode into the Peloponnesian War.

Over the centuries, violent earthquakes and generations of souvenir hunters erased almost all vestiges of ancient brilliance in the Ionians. Its most vivid relic is the mysterious grinning Gorgon in a temple dating to the sixth century B.C. in Corfu.

The Ionians were little affected by the rise and fall of Macedonia, but Corfu was the first Greek city to succumb to the Romans. After proclaiming themselves "Protectors of the Freedom of Greece," the Romans parceled the islands up into private estates. They used Corfu as a playground, the way tourists do today. Nero stopped off to give a song and dance recital, Antony married Octavia there (and then jilted her in favor of Cleopatra), and Augustus amassed his fleet offshore for the battle of Actium (where he defeated Antony), while Cicero's ashes were entombed in Zakynthos. In their enthusiasm for all things Greek, the Romans adopted the sophisticated local cuisine—which had come a long way from the spitted ox or lamb so dear to the warriors at Troy. Not satisfied with the delicate fish soups and stuffed vegetables perfected by the Greeks, they sprinkled their lentils with precious stones and sent explorers to the far reaches of their empire to bring back ever more exotic morsels. Over the years, Roman chefs so disguised their dishes with contrasting spices and elaborate artifice that guests at a banquet no longer had any idea what they were eating or even what part of the meal was edible. After Rome fell, it was back to bread, gruel, and onions for the islanders, but hints of Roman recipes still live on in sweet and sour dishes combining vinegar and currants.

FROM BYZANTINE TERRITORIES
TO FEUDAL FIEFS

With the collapse of the Western Roman Empire, the Ionian Islands automatically became part of the Byzantine Empire, its successor. It is in Byzantium, most of all, that one finds the roots of Ionian and Greek cooking. Sauces bound with eggs and perked up with lemons, vegetables stewed in olive oil, and a variety of methods for preparing fish all seem to be part of this heritage.

Although it is often impossible to say for certain where the Byzantine, Arab, Turkish, and Italian influences begin and end in much of the Mediterranean's eating habits, most of them certainly impinged on the Ionians. In the centuries between the fall of Rome and the Venetian occupation of Corfu some nine hundred years later,

Byzantine church of Sts. Jason and Sosipater, Corfu

the islands seem to have attracted every one of the trading or land-seeking powers and would-be powers that cruised the enclosed sea. Far away in Constantinople, the emperors felt their control waning over the islands on the western horizon of their far-flung empire. In exchange for trading privileges, they enlisted the help of a former Byzantine province in defending the Ionians against these threats.

By the twelfth century, the Serene Republic of Venice had established herself as the superpower of the age. Her most famous subject, Marco Polo, had brought back fabulous tales of China, its unimaginable wealth and delectable noodles. It was not long before a good portion of the Silk Road led straight into the holds of Venetian ships. Always guided by the profit motive, the Doge and his admirals turned on their former ally. They diverted the Crusaders (not unwillingly) from routing the infidel from Jerusalem and in 1204 engineered the capture of the greatest city in the world. With Constantinople in Frankish hands, Venice supervised the parceling out of the vast Byzantine Empire, choosing the most advantageous

Marco Polo brings silk and spaghetti from China

bits for herself, including Crete, several key Aegean islands, and a number of strategic ports in the Peloponnese. While nominally in command of the Ionian Islands, the Doge left them in the hands of the Italian princes already installed there.

THE LATINS IN THE LEVANT

Meanwhile, nobles from southern Italy had taken advantage of the power vacuum in Cephalonia and Zakynthos, which they renamed Zante, and soon extended their rule to Ithaca and Lefkada, which they christened Santa Maura. On Kythera, on the other hand, a Venetian family called Venieri, declaring their descent from Venus herself, ensconced themselves as the only truly legitimate governors of her birthplace.

Corfu's fate was not as smooth. After a succession of ever weaker rulers could not protect her from pirates and Latin (Italian, Catalan, French) adventurers, in 1386 she turned to Venice as the only power strong enough to fend them off.

Gate to the Old Fort

In those days, most of the population lived within the walls of the Old Fort built upon the twin-peaked promontory in the middle of the island's east coast. This Citadel *"ton Koryfón"* (of the Peaks) gave both the town and island of Kerkyra its western name. The Venetians agreed to repair and expand the fort in exchange for the right to levy taxes. In time, this right mushroomed into total control of the economy.

Ironically, by weakening the Byzantine Empire, the Venetians and their European cohorts ultimately made it much easier for a Turkic tribe to consolidate their strength in the East and threaten Venetian interests. Though the Greeks had won back Constantinople and much of the rest of their territory, before long the Ottomans wrested it from them again. In so doing, they also endangered the vast Venetian trade empire. After the Turkish conquest of Constantinople in 1453, the Serene Republic and the Sublime Porte were to fight seven wars over the next two and a half centuries. But both states were careful to keep their lucrative business relationships separate from military matters. Within fifty years, Venice had managed to win the other Ionian Islands, with the exception of Lefkada. In the end, they were all she had left.

Repeated wars eventually exhausted Venice, and Mediterranean trade began to dwindle as new markets opened with the discovery of the New World and sea routes to the Orient. But Venice did not let go of her Ionian possessions until Napoleon's army gave her the coup de grace. While the rest of Greece was kept backward under Ottoman rule, the Ionians were welcoming western ships and enjoying prosperity. Only Lefkada experienced the Turkish occupation for any appreciable period—about two hundred years—and the Venetian heritage there is paler as a result.

LIFE IN THE VENETIAN COLONIES

When Venice took over the Ionian Islands—which she called Le Isole di Levante—she was just beginning to totter from her pinnacle. Even so, six immense trading fleets left the lagoon every year for the eastern Mediterranean ports, taking on cargoes of wine, olive oil, and currants from Greece as well as ivory, brocades, silks, cottons, spices, apes, peacocks, dyes, scents, and gold from China, Persia, and India. The Ionian islands became Venetian naval bases and depots until Venice lost its possessions on the mainland.

To compensate for the loss of these markets, Venice made some decisions that were to change the islands' very landscape. Using the

Venetian trading ship

carrot rather than the stick, the Doge offered to pay twelve gold pieces for every hundred olive trees planted. While saplings sprouted rapidly on all the islands, in Corfu they crowded out many of the vineyards and wheatfields, making the island into one enormous olive grove. By the end of the seventeenth century, Corfu could boast two million trees and was exporting sixty thousand barrels of oil every other year. In time, this devotion to a one-crop economy meant that Corfu could no longer feed its people; it became necessary to import grain, meat, and vegetables—an ironic situation for the fertile garden of Alcinoos.

In Zakynthos and Cephalonia, Venice reintroduced another crop, the currant, named after its birthplace, Corinth, then under Turkish rule. In 1685, an English traveler named Wheler wrote that Zakynthos was a "Golden island [and] . . . truly merits that name from the Venetians who draw so much Gold by the currant trade." Then as now, they grew "in a most pleasant plain behind the Castle, divided into vineyards mixed with Olive, Cypress-trees and Summer-houses of pleasure." Wheler describes how they were dried and stored, mentioning that the English, French, and Dutch all maintained consuls and merchants there. "The English have the chief Trade here, and good reason they should: For I believe they eat six times as much of their fruit as both France and Holland do. The Zantiots have not long known what we do with them; but have been persaded [*sic*] that we use them only to Dye Cloth with; and are yet strangers to the luxury of Christmas pies, Plum-potage, Cake and Puddings, etc." Curiously, all the islanders remained "strangers" to these dishes until they saw the English eating them in the nineteenth century.

To govern their islands, the Venetians encouraged the feudal system already in force. They appointed one of their own noblemen as *Provveditore Generale* to oversee the governors of the other islands from his headquarters in Corfu. And while Venetians controlled some of the more sensitive positions—such as chief of police and salt commissioner (we tend to forget how vital salt was in those days; there are salt pans, *alykes*, on all the main islands)—the other admin-

Gathering salt

istrative posts were held in rotation by members of a council elected from among each island's aristocracy. The names of these noble families were registered in a Golden Book (*Libro d'Oro*). The privileges that went along with the honor of election to the council implied certain restrictions that molded their way of life.

In order to serve, noblemen had to reside in town and were not permitted to engage in trade. As a result, they tended to leave the management of their estates to tenant farmers, while they spent their days politicking, socializing, and gambling. The Venetians allowed no public schools on the islands, but Padua University was open to any Ionian youth who wanted to go. To discourage their colonial students from serious study, Padua professors had instructions to issue them diplomas without requiring examinations. Even so, they returned to form an educated, cultivated upper class that emulated Venetian ways and had no real occupation.

At the other end of the spectrum, the mass of the peasantry had no contact at all with the Venetians and lived very close to poverty. The peasants spoke only Greek; the aristocrats Italian, using their native tongue solely to communicate with their servants. Even today the Ionian vocabulary contains hundreds of Italian words; grandmothers are called "nonna," bacon "pancetta," and so forth.

The trade boom of the sixteenth and seventeenth centuries created a new class of merchants with money to spend. The urban population had long since felt safe enough to leave the precincts of the castles, and now they poured their new money into magnificent homes and churches—elegant baroque edifices with no resemblance to the unassuming Byzantine chapels of the previous centuries. In the meantime, Cretan artists fleeing the Ottoman conquest of their own land found patrons and plenty of walls to decorate in the Ionian Islands. Full-bodied figures and natural landscapes provided the inspiration for what developed into the Ionian School of Painting. The combination of lovely countryside and exquisite buildings won Zakynthos the epithet *Zante, fior' di Levante* (flower of the Levant).

The ascendancy of the middle class paralleled a decline in the Venetian ability to govern. For the first century and a half, the governors had taken their duties seriously; they toured the islands, listened to complaints, and rectified them. But as perennial warfare and shrinking trade drained the Venetian treasury and decadence began to flourish in the Republic, the islands were sent less capable, relatively impoverished nobles for whom corruption was the only way to survive. Law and order slowly gave way to bribes and blood feuds until murders became routine and anyone with a vegetable garden feared for "its very soil," much less its cabbages. By the eighteenth century, the *Provedditore Generale* in Corfu was reduced to living in

Remains of Venetian arsenal, Corfu

quarters furnished by a rental company, which also supplied the red carpets for special occasions and the linen and cutlery for state dinners.

Every gentleman invited to such functions knew that these galas had a price: each was expected to leave an order or cash payment for either olive oil or currants slipped neatly under his plate. (In Cephalonia, however, one man had discovered the secret to a free meal. According to Viscount Kirkwall, an English lord who lived on the islands in the 1860s, this by-then legendary gentleman regularly showed up for dinner at the governor's residence, having first checked with the chef that the menu was to his liking. The governor, whose poor memory was notorious, could never remember whether he'd been invited or not and courteously received him.)

Once upon a time Venetian cuisine was touted as the finest in the world. Their concoctions of game, rococo salads, and "architectural pastries" were famous. There is little evidence of this aspect of their heritage in the Ionian Islands today except the extraordinary pie known as *Venetziániko pastítsio* (see page 168). The anchovies, sage, and rosemary so common as seasonings in Venetian cooking are not apparent in Ionian cuisine. But we should not overlook that it was Venice who introduced the Ionians to the main New World vegetable we have come to associate with Mediterranean cooking—the tomato—not to mention peppers, string beans, corn, and pumpkins, still sometimes called Venetian squash in Zakynthos.

Later, it was said caustically that the pride of Venetian cookery was the hard biscuit, which resisted all incursions by marauding weevils. James Morris reported that some left in Crete in 1665 were still edible in 1821. Called *paximádia*, these are ubiquitous in many variations throughout Greece (see pages 203–204).

THE LAST YEARS OF VENETIAN RULE

Many of our ideas of what the islands and islanders were like during the final years of the Venetian occupation come from English writers of the early nineteenth century. They tell us that the theater—the Commedia dell'Arte—and the opera were all the rage in Corfu, Cephalonia, and Zakynthos, though gossip and card playing often

took precedence over the happenings on stage. Women began to appear in public, wearing masks at first. They later adopted European dress, unlike their country cousins, who in the mountain villages of Corfu and Lefkada can still be found wearing traditional costumes and headdresses. In Cephalonia, modesty ruled at the cobbler's, however. Kirkwall relates that their shops were outfitted with special doors with holes through which young women would pass their feet to be measured for shoes.

The Venetian lifestyle was so entrenched that long into the British Protectorate, Italian remained one of the official languages, and Italian habits and manners were still very evident well into the twentieth century. Given the English suspicion of all things foreign coupled with their feelings of superiority at having supplanted Venice as the world's greatest maritime power, some writers complained about Ionian laziness and reluctance to take things seriously. They called these "Venetian vices."

Other, more sympathetic, writers like Kirkwall were able to see "that the idleness of which the Ionians have been accused was less their fault than their misfortune," imposed by a system that prohibited them from having a profession. Charles James Napier, the first governor of Cephalonia and later viceroy in India, loved its people and, unlike the majority of his countrymen, was fluent in both Greek and Italian; he therefore knew the Ionians well enough to defend them fairly. In 1833, he wrote that ". . . the richer classes are lively and agreeable in their manners; and among the men, many are well informed. The women possess both beauty and wit, in abundance. . . . The poor are not less industrious than other southern nations; and an extraordinary degree of intelligence characterizes all ranks."

Viewing the criticism from the other side, one Corfiot aristocrat once explained that "the Ionian islanders were occupied for so long, they were bound to find a way of dealing with their occupiers. They learned how to survive and prosper by becoming flatterers and letting the foreigners do all the work."

WINDS OF CHANGE

In 1797 as Napoleon Bonaparte's soldiers marched into Venice, he turned his attention southwards, planning his Egyptian campaign. Finding the islands of Corfu, Zakynthos, and Cephalonia "more interesting than the whole of Italy," he sent two thousand troops to occupy them, which they did with very little difficulty. In those early days of *Liberté, Fraternité, Egalité,* the French won the peasants' hearts by burning the detested *Libro d'Oro.* The aristocrats were less enthusiastic.

The French also brought with them such exciting novelties as the printing press, which the intelligentsia welcomed; the potato, which no one would touch; and the turkey, called in Greek *gallopoúla* or "French bird." This legacy lives on in Lefkada. When they shop for their Christmas turkey, the Lefkadians say "we're going to seize the Frenchman" (*na piásoume ton gállo*).

Viewing Napoleon's progress through Europe with alarm, Russia—which, being Orthodox, had become a focus for Greek aspirations to freedom—formed an unlikely alliance with the Ottoman Empire, her long-time enemy. The two nations succeeded in temporarily ousting the French, and they set up a paper federation called The Septinsular Republic, which enjoyed Russian protection and paid tribute to the Sultan. It was during this time that the term "Ionian Islands" first came into use; the Greeks, however, always call them the Eptanisa or Seven Islands.

The Liston Arcade, Corfu

Just one recipe exists from this period. Unearthed by food writer Diane Kochilas, it calls for fish fried in butter and then cooked with potatoes and milk. In those days, most Corfiots would have been horrified at using such a rare commodity as butter for frying. The potato was still an object of suspicion, and, even today, combining milk with fish is frowned upon by many Greeks.

The years before Waterloo were confusing for the Ionians. Though autocratic and short-lived, their illusory republic gave them a taste for freedom, fanned by the democratic ideas introduced by the French, who regained Corfu in 1807. In addition to attempting to introduce modern farming techniques and public works, the French constructed the Liston, the elegant arcade that separates the park known as the *Spianáda,* or "Esplanade," from the town. A *Rue de Rivoli* look-alike, the arcade is said to have taken its name from the fact that only the gentry, those on the List, were permitted to walk under it.

When Napoleon finally lost the war, the Great Powers—Great Britain, Prussia, Austria, and Russia—met in Vienna in 1815 to decide, among other things, what to do with the Ionian Islands. At that time, a young Corfiot named John Capodistrias was chief of the Russian delegation and spoke for the Greek cause. Failing to secure

Russian protection, Capodistrias convinced the Congress to assign the islands to Britain. As Kirkwall writes, "They were thus set up as the free and independent United States of the Ionian Islands under the immediate and exclusive protection of the king of Great Britain, though no sane man can believe that the Congress of Sovereigns had any intention of setting up a real republic in the long-distracted and turbulent Ionian Islands." Capodistrias went back to Russia and later returned to Greece as the first governor of the free nation in 1828.

ROADS, STABILITY, AND CRICKET

The English ruled the islands until 1864, providing safety, schools, roads, waterworks, and palaces. They also planted vegetable gardens, tended by Maltese or Italian gardeners. Several writers of the time noted with disbelief that many of the local population, especially in Lefkada, preferred buying their vegetables in the marketplace to growing their own. No explanation was forthcoming.

Their first Lord High Commissioner, Thomas Maitland, otherwise known as King Tom for his autocratic ways, managed "almost" to put an end to the murders that had replaced justice to the tune of about one per day at the end of the Venetian occupation. And the founding of the Ionian Academy by Lord Guilford meant that young men no longer had to go abroad to study. But the English perpetuated

The Rotunda of Corfu

two of the Venetians' injustices: they provided no opening for educated Greeks to find a career outside law or medicine, and they allowed no freedom of expression.

During the Greek War of Independence (1821-1828), British insistence on Ionian noninvolvement enraged the islanders even as Lord Byron was plotting his Philhellene maneuvers from Cephalonia. After the mainland won its independence from the Turks, this injunction became increasingly offensive as many Ionian citizens, tired of more than six hundred years of foreign domination, longed for union with a free Greece. There were bloody rebellions on all the major islands, though some Anglophiles sided with the Protectorate. In most cases, however, Italian manners and Victorian frock coats and bustles concealed a spirit that was deeply Greek.

Finally, in 1864, weary of the mounting unrest and dwindling profits, Queen Victoria's government signed the islands over to Greece—the first time in history that any country surrendered a possession without a war. The English left behind an appreciation for cricket, ginger beer, marching bands, and British puddings.

GREEK AT LAST

Without the guaranteed British market, the Ionian economy plummeted dramatically as it tried to shift its focus to Athens. Many of the poorer residents of Ithaca, Cephalonia, and Kythera were eventually forced to emigrate to the United States, Africa, or Australia—where there are now more Kytherans than there are on Kythera itself.

Some glamorous figures still frequented the islands: the Greek royal family summered in Corfu, and Elizabeth, the Empress of Austria, built the Achilleion Palace there. After her assassination, Kaiser Wilhelm II bought it, and, for a month every summer until 1914, moved the whole Berlin court there. The Murray's guidebooks of the day contain detailed instructions for sportsmen who wish to take advantage of the splendid shooting in the area; the Mediterranean fleet paid an annual visit, and, on Ithaca's highest mountain, Heinrich Schliemann caused great excitement by excavating "Ulysses' palace," which has since proved several centuries too new.

Stairs to the Achilleion

Cultural life on the islands continued to thrive, despite the merger of the Ionian Academy with Athens University, which effectively meant the former ceased to exist. During the Protectorate, Zakynthos had given birth to three internationally known poets: Ugo Foscolo, who wrote in Italian; Andreas Kalvos; and Dionysios Solomos, author of the Greek national anthem, "Hymn to Liberty," set to music composed by Nikolaos Mantzaros, a Corfiot. Painters and architects were granted commissions, philharmonic societies sprouted, and operas were performed on the three larger islands until 1939. Ionian politicians moved to the national stage, careful to remind the mainlanders of their "superior heritage."

Nevertheless, in spite of itself, the Ionians became a backwater, its prosperous, sophisticated past fading into the stuff of dreams and memories. Some of tangible remains of their glory days were destroyed by man: in 1923 Mussolini had Corfu shelled in unjust retaliation for a now-forgotten incident; during the Second World War Allied—as well as Nazi—bombing caused a fire that wiped out a third of Corfu Town, in addition to inflicting damage on Zakynthos and Cephalonia. But no humans can be blamed for the most devastating eradication of the past.

In 1948, Lefkada's antiseismic two-story dwellings crumbled in an earthquake, killing two people. Five years later, an even stronger quake razed 70 percent of the buildings in Cephalonia, Ithaca, and Zakynthos, leaving at least six hundred dead and seventy-five thousand homeless. Half their populations fled and never returned.

Earthquakes have always been common in the southern Ionians, which lie astride not one but two major faults. In earlier centuries, travelers had noted that "the palaces [were] more safe than ornamental," not very high due to frequent tremors, "which the locals make little or nothing of." But the 1953 earthquake raged on an unprecedented scale. In just a few seconds centuries-old towns and villages ceased to exist, while fires swept through Zakynthos Town, completing the disaster. The Army Corps of Engineers dynamited and bulldozed the wreckage, erecting solid but charmless buildings in their place. In Zakynthos, the arcades and some facades were lovingly reconstructed, the churches rebuilt stone by stone. But they resemble a stage set and we can only imagine what the prettiest town in Venice's empire must really have been like.

Before the Second World War, however, a seemingly insignificant event—destined to have momentous consequences for all the Ionians—occurred in Corfu: the Durrell family took up residence. With their books, *Prospero's Cell* and *My Family and Other Animals*, Larry and Gerry Durrell painted such charming portraits of Corfu and the Corfiots that hundreds of readers flocked to see for themselves. Those hundreds have turned to hundreds of thousands who have spilled over into all the islands, in something that in July and August can be compared to yet another foreign occupation. Most of the visitors hardly ever get a chance to taste real Ionian cooking. This book aims to reveal what they are missing.

DAILY LIFE ⁰N THE ISLANDS

UNDER THE BRITISH

In 1872, Murray's *Handbook for Travellers in Greece* described Corfu as "a sort of geographical mosaic to which many countries of Europe have contributed colors. . . . A stranger will hear Italian from the native gentry, Greek from the peasants, Arabic from the Maltese grooms and gardeners, Albanian from the white-kilted mountaineers of the opposite coast."

Both during the years as a British Protectorate (1815–1864) and well into the twentieth century, this mosaic made the city extraordinarily lively, abuzz from early morning until just before dawn. By day the main streets were bustling with pedestrians and carriages, while urchins darted among them beseeching the English "lords" for "fardings, fardings." Englishmen groaned that the "excessive politeness of the Ionians required you to have your hat perpetually in your hands. People walk in the streets and expect the carriages to make way for them." (Anyone who has tried to maneuver a car in a Greek town knows that this mentality still prevails.)

Shopping was the principal undertaking of the daytime hours. A. H. Tsitsas, in his delightful portrait of old Corfu, says that at the end of the eighteenth century—and presumably well into British rule—there were over sixty shops or *botteghe* in the town center. By far the most numerous were the *boutélia* or olive oil storehouses, which performed all the functions of banks. As the island's only export product, olive oil was handled like currency: bought, sold, loaned, and speculated upon. The second most common establishments were the taverns, followed by the green grocers, cheese shops, grocers, and barbers. In those days, the Ionian barber was the next best thing to a surgeon; he even kept a jar of leeches on his shelf for bleeding away excessive humors. There were also four pharmacies (*spicerie*); three bakeries (called *foúrnoi* or ovens in Greek), where people would also take their food to be baked after the bakers' bread had been removed—a practice that continues today; two cafés; a shoe-maker; a wigmaker; a potter; and a *manestropoieíon*, the pasta maker. In the islands today *manéstra* is still the generic term for small types of pasta. In the main towns of the other islands the shops—called by a characteristically Ionian hotchpotch of Greek and Italian words—followed a similar pattern on a smaller scale.

Even after shopping hours, the streets teemed with noisy pedestrians from about eight in the evening until three or four in the morning. Groups of young men would stroll about singing loudly for much of the night, a custom tolerated provided they did not linger in any one spot and disturb one neighborhood's sleep exclusively. Apart from rowdy tavern patrons, there were the serenaders whose courtship rites did not begin until after midnight. Then the swain and his friends would take up their positions under the chosen damsel's window, strumming tender ballads (*cantádes*) on their guitars and mandolins, impatient for a sign—even the shutters opening a crack was considered encouragement enough. This practice continued until the Second World War in all the main towns, with romance reaching its peak in Zakynthos when an ardent lover hoisted his piano onto a cart and rolled it below his beloved's balcony.

WINING AND DINING

The upper social echelons in the past century did not appear to need much sleep either. In the evenings there were often large parties and balls, held by the British. The Greeks rarely reciprocated, much to their hosts' consternation. As Viscount Kirkwall complained, "It is rare for an Ionian to have a dinner party—how, where, when [they dine] has usually remained a masonic secret for Englishmen."

Confusion could also arise when they did, as Tertius Kendrick bemoaned after a dinner given in Corfu in 1822 for British officers by a certain Count A: "The dinner was not laid out on the table, as is the custom of France or England [and very much of Greece today]; a number of domestics brought in various meats, always a single plate at a time, which was placed before the guest, who knew not, by this mode, what was to come next. This put our English gentry into a disagreeable situation, as custom obliges one to partake of each entremet. After a change of nine times, a domestic, apparently the maggior d'omo, advanced to the head of the table, and declared dinner to be finished. A dessert replaced the substantial viands, consisting of fruit common to the island, such as green figs, grapes, currants, etc." The dinner was accompanied by wines from the count's estate as well as French wines and followed by coffee and a liqueur called *rosolio*.

Kendrick attended another party during his visit where he witnessed a curious custom from Venetian times. "The Corfuiote [*sic*] lady opposite to me, also took care not to rise empty handed. She had obtained a large sheet of paper into which were put all manner of 'good things,' then carefully wrapt up and carried off by her at an appropriate time. Her rapacious grasp was not to be checked in spite of special observations and hints from her brother, who said it was not 'secondo il modo inglese di far cosi' [not the English way to do such things]. Her reply was 'Taci bestia—andate a ballare.' [Shut up, you beast, go and dance.]"

Forty years later, guests at a Cephalonian wedding were urged to be similarly greedy: "First ices were passed and then sugarplums— interminable baskets of white and colored sugarplums of various shapes and sizes. . . . The etiquette was rigid, and applied to old as well as to young. The rule was to fill your coat, waistcoat, and breeches pockets, as also your pocket handkerchief (in short every available receptacle), with these bonbons. For politeness sake, [Viscount Kirkwall] was ready to do everything—except swallow them. . . . 50£ sterling had been paid by the hostess on these strange comestibles."

THE PERILS AND BENEFITS
OF NATIVE COOKERY

By and large, the English stationed on the islands made no attempt to adjust their diet to the mild Mediterranean climate. When they ventured into the countryside as guests of an Ionian landowner, they invariably took their chefs along. The host would provide the raw materials, which the chef would then prepare in a safe, familiar manner. "Thus you escape the oil and garlic flavor which usually permeates all native cookery." Kirkwall also reports that whereas "excellent cooks were to be had in Corfu, in Cephalonia tolerable fresh meat was very difficult to procure, and the cooks had been trained in a school of grease, garlic and oil."

A Corfiot noble named Emmanuel Theotokis presented the Ionian diet more favorably: "The people consume little meat; fresh or smoked fish, cured olives, or cheese, vegetables, corncakes, pumpkins, calabash, dried or fresh fruit, furnish them with a healthy, inexpensive meal. The leisure classes consume more meat and they pay for it; for, in this climate, it is heavy and indigestible for delicate and sedentary people, of which this class generally consists."

Leaving dietary differences aside, another common English complaint was that young Greek women rarely appeared at their parties. Kirkwall lamented that "the Greeks do not appear to fully understand . . . that general preference for the society of the fair sex so prevalent in the west of Europe." (Though it is highly likely they understood only too well! Lafcadio Hearn's father was one soldier who managed to court his Lefkadian wife through the chaperone barrier.) So desperate were the young officers in Argostoli for the sight of a female face that they staged a parade riding bell-bedecked donkeys backward through the streets to catch a glimpse of the ladies. Everyone rushed to their balconies to see the cause of the

The rooftops of Corfu town, the old fort in distance

commotion, and the young men got their wish. In Zakynthos and Corfu, on the contrary, many of the ladies spoke English well and mixed cordially with English society, but even there unmarried women were confined to the home.

Apart from such minor complaints, the English enjoyed their days in the Ionian, where peasants would offer them grapes without expecting payment and any trip to the smaller islands was met with unstinting hospitality. For years afterwards, countless beauty spots in the countryside were littered with oyster shells and broken champagne bottles, souvenirs of that peculiarly English institution, the picnic. It is true that riots occasionally disturbed the peace, especially in "unruly Cephalonia," but for the most part the British could look back on their fifty-odd years with nostalgia.

ABIDING GREEK PLEASURES

While the English in Corfu entertained themselves by conducting paper chases through the countryside, attending horse races, or watching cricket, what the Greeks most enjoyed were the festivals — *panigýria* — that took place on saints' days and holidays. But an American visitor named Tuckerman spoke for many of the British when he rebuked the Ionians for being "excessively fond of amusement and display. . . . The number of holidays seriously interferes with the industry and prosperity of the people. Scarcely two thirds of the year are occupied by working days. [Then] the people give themselves wholly up to pleasure; which . . . consists in an unusual modicum of bell-ringing, martial music, discharges of cannon, perambulation in the streets in holiday attire and fireworks."

On such occasions, the streets or squares were filled with small booths selling all kinds of cheap wares, refreshments, and religious memorabilia while marching bands performing rollicking music. During the nineteenth century and up until the Second World War, these celebrations were almost the only events where the townspeople and peasants, upper, middle, and lower classes, ever mingled. They also performed the function of a marriage bazaar (*nyfopázaro*), as they gave young men and women the chance to flirt with a minimum of surveillance—everyone had too good a time to pay much attention. The marriage broker, always busier after a *panigýri*, was sent swiftly to arrange the elaborate negotiations over dowry and land that settled a couple's fate. A girl was lucky if she married the man of her choice and not some rich but elderly tyrant her father preferred.

A rural *panigýri*, held in a remote chapel opened just once a year in honor of its saint, is still a bucolic event. Even Odysseus would not feel out of place among the throng, for once mass is over, the Christian element vanishes. Lambs are roasted on the spit; wine is guzzled without restraint; and the men, women, and sometimes children dance, often separately, performing rigidly prescribed steps whose origin may be as old as the bonfire. The only significant change since the days of yore is in the dress. Gone are the magnificent women's feast-day costumes. In the past, the unmarried girls tried to look their loveliest but the newly married were even more arresting. They would arrive on horseback, seated atop several layers of multicolored blankets, wearing resplendent full-length skirts, gold-trimmed bodices, embroidered blouses with puffed sleeves, and draped from head to waist with heavy gold or silver head ornaments, earrings, necklaces, brooches, and belts.

British soldiers riding donkeys backwards up the streets of Argostoli

A city fair was always more commercial than a rural *panigýri*, but though the toys and trinkets are plastic now, some of the smells and treats have been the same for centuries. Forget the ubiquitous cotton candy and popcorn; here you will find vendors stirring almonds bubbling in red syrup—the crunchy *mándoles* or pralines that are a Cephalonian specialty—pouring pots of viscous, sesame-laced honey onto marble slabs to cool into tooth-threatening *pastélli*, or slicing *fritoúres*, wedges of semolina fried in oil and sprinkled with sugar and cinnamon.

PATRON SAINTS AND PROCESSIONS

For true pomp and ceremony, the celebrations in honor of the patron saints of the three main islands were—and still are—the most impressive of all. They are, however, harder for foreigners to appreciate: the islanders freely exhibit their devotion to what is essentially a mummy, albeit gold-bedecked. Four times a year in Corfu and twice in Zakynthos and Cephalonia, the shrivelled but sumptuously dressed body of the saint is removed from its heavy casket, placed in a kind of glass-paneled sedan chair, and taken on a walk around his town or monastery so that all can pay homage. This formal procession can perhaps be compared to a small-town Fourth of July parade: everyone—from local government officials, the clergical hierarchy, soldiers, sailors, and marines to scouts and school children in shiny white shirts and blue trousers or skirts—joins in, all stepping smartly to marches played by the island's philharmonic societies with what looks like the whole population in attendance.

Sixty years ago, Lawrence Durrell found the uniforms and vestments so colorful, the traditional gala peasant costumes so dazzling, that he described the processions as akin to "a moving flower bed." They do not seem to have impressed Private Wheeler, whose letters from Corfu in the 1820s reveal his condescending view of the proceedings: "After the whole of the town had been perambulated, and half the sick had received their death stroke from the powerful rays of the sun, the Saint is once more stood up by the altar, when the old trade of kissing his boots, and dropping money in the dish again begins, and is continued until late the next day, when the holy person is again entombed."

To the Ionian islanders, however, their saints are not only sacred, they are intimate friends who appear in their dreams, whom they scold when their problems are not solved, and upon whom they lavish gifts when their prayers are granted. Corfu's St. Spýridon was a fourth-century Cypriot bishop esteemed for his intelligence and humanity. After his death his body exhibited his beatitude by emitting a flowery perfume rather than decomposing. A priest with an eye for relics salvaged the saint, along with the body of the less renowned St. Theodora, from the Turkish sack of Constantinople and allegedly transported them on muleback over the mainland to Corfu in 1456. St. Spýridon was a credit to his owner from the start as believers from as far away as the Peloponnese and the Aegean sought the saint's protection and left donations. By the mid-sixteenth century, he had worked his first major miracle—saving the island from famine. This and his three other official miracles—saving the island from a Turkish siege and two outbreaks of the plague—are commemorated by processions.

Zakynthos has St. Dionýsios and Cephalonia St. Yerásimos, both of whom lived more a thousand years after St. Spýridon. They each have two processions per year. When the saints are not on parade, people file in and out of the churches containing their sarcophagi. Fragile widows swathed in black, tattooed teenagers in mini-skirts, and gentlemen in business suits, all wait their turn to kiss the enamel panels on the bronze casket lids. And every year one

woman is chosen to make each saint a pair of embroidered slippers. It is said that they wear them out going about the islands at night listening to prayers.

All three saints are held in such high regard that at least half the males on each island are named after its patron saint. This can become confusing, for if you call out "Spyro," to take one example, on a crowded street in Corfu, dozens of heads will look round.

CHRISTMAS

Until twentieth-century commercialism penetrated Greek customs in the 1960s and 1970s, Christmas on the mainland was merely an important name day—an occasion for people called Christos or Christina to entertain. In the already westernized Ionian Islands, however, Christmas was a three-day holiday with a two-month build-up.

In Corfu, the first harbingers of the holiday season were the *tiganítes* or holeless doughnuts fried in huge copper cauldrons of sizzling oil under the arcades in the center of town. The first cauldrons appeared on the evening of October 20th, St. Yerasimos's day, the last ones vanished the day after St. Spyridon's on December 12th. As St. Spyridon's day approached, more and more cauldrons would be bubbling there, and more and more passersby would walk home with a paper cornet of the crunchy fritters dusted with sugar and cinnamon. The tradition is still alive but now it starts later in the fall and there are fewer vendors.

Because daily life was regulated by the saints, St. Philip's on November 14th marked the beginning of the pre-Christmas fasting period, forty days of self-denial as stringent as Lent. This was the day the farmers and butchers would slaughter their pigs and start to make salamis, sausages, and pancetta, as well as smoked filets and hams for the Christmas table.

As Tsitsas recalls in his booklet on Corfu before the Second World War, the atmosphere became more festive in early December around the days of the popular saints, Barbara, Savvas, and Nicholas, on the 4th, 5th, and 6th of December. Even the most pious fasters relaxed their rules at what the Corfiots call "the first Christmas" on December 12th. This was the time to worship their own beloved St. Spýridon and every family that could afford it sat down to turkey and *avgolémono* (egg-lemon) soup (see page 84). During this period the church bells seemed to ring nonstop. The English used to complain vehemently about Ionian bell-ringing, which they called "auricular torture" or the "tintinnabulary enemy," but it was music to the ears of the locals.

Christmas at the butcher's

Around this time, the normally hectic bustle became even more ebullient with pre-Christmas shopping. Greetings shouted over the stentorian cries of the vendors and the clanging bells ricocheted through the arcades. As Tsitsas tells us, the shopkeepers outdid themselves with extravaganzas of decoration. The butchers draped evergreen boughs over the hams, baby lambs, and sausage garlands dangling above their chopping blocks and left unplucked tail feathers as a decorous veil for turkey posteriors; hampers of walnuts, chestnuts, dried figs, prunes, and glistening oranges extended so far into the narrow alleyways they made walking difficult; and pyramids of cheeses, imported and local, rose above myrtle-bedecked salamis and charcuterie. Adding to the ferment were the strolling nut sellers and hawkers of small items, who would dart under the arcades when Corfu's notorious rains poured down, consoling themselves and the crowds by singing carols in perfect harmony. In the evenings after church and after practice, members of Corfu's many philharmonic societies would stroll round town crooning and playing more carols. Carol singing continued throughout the season, peaking on

Christmas Eve, New Year's Eve, and Epiphany. In all the Ionians, the carols are set to western-style melodies and have nothing in common with the nasal chants of the mainland *kálanda*.

Meanwhile, housewives on all the islands carried out a virtual spring cleaning in preparation for the Christmas feasting. Besides polishing to a brilliant sheen the silver and the copper pots and molds that in those days covered the kitchen walls, they even white-washed the kitchen itself. Their final task was to set the dining room table with a white damask cloth taken from the dowry chest. Apart from meal times, a carafe of wine and bowls of Christmas *kouloúria* or biscuits stood there in permanent readiness for impromptu visitors. As for decoration, some houses—even in Ithaca—boasted one very un-Greek feature: a Christmas tree, trimmed with homemade ornaments, tufts of cotton masquerading as snow, and candles. Buckets of sand and water stood concealed nearby in case of fire. In the Aegean and around Athens, the traditional Christmas ornament is a model fishing caïque set in a central position and surrounded by gifts. Only in the cities has the Christmas tree become a status symbol over the past twenty years. But whether the presents are under a tree or a boat, most Greeks, Ionians included, do not open them until the New Year.

On the first day of Christmas in Corfu and Zakynthos, egg-lemon soup was the prescribed dish, followed by the beef used to make the broth. The more prosperous might also serve a haunch of roast pork, studded with garlic, or roast lamb embellished with the first tender artichokes. The turkey did not appear until the second day. It frequently shared pride of place with the gargantuan *Venetziániko pastítsio*, a pie of sorts containing everything from game to meatballs and mortadella sandwiched between two layers of macaroni encased within a sweet crust (see page 168). Supplementing every meal were peppery salamis, the Corfiot smoked pork fillet known as *noúmboulo*, cheeses, and a relish called *moustárda*, a piquant quince marmalade. For dessert, although some families with English connections would serve plum pudding, more common were fresh and dried fruit, including the confection known as *sykomaïda*. Translated as fig bread, it also contains walnuts, pepper, and ouzo.

Needless to say, this groaning board did not grace the humbler houses of the poorer country people, who might have had an old hen or a joint of lamb, but for whom even a stew of salt cod would have been a treat after their usual sparse vegetarian fare.

The Zakynthians preceded the feasting with a modest meal of boiled broccoli on Christmas Eve, the last day of the fasting period. Even nowadays shoppers scurry round town with trimmed bunches of the purple-sprouting variety spilling out of their carts or tied to the backs of their motorbikes. Christmas Eve is also when households cut their *kouloúra*, a large cake shaped like a ring and containing a coin for luck. It is made of the same dough as Zakynthos's *Christópsomo* or Christmas bread, a kind of spice cake with nuts and raisins resembling the Italian *panettone* (see page 202). In the country-side you can always tell when a family is cutting the *kouloúra* from the fusillades fired from the farmers' shotguns. As for the island's turkeys, they were and are particularly juicy, for they feed on windfall olives. In the old days the farmers used to bring their live turkeys to town, filling the streets with gobbling while buyers selected them in full feather.

As for Ionian New Year's customs, there is little that distinguishes them from the celebrations in the rest of Greece. Typically, the eve is a time set aside for card playing for luck. The day itself, dedicated to St. Vassilios, the Greek Santa Claus, is when families get together for present giving, more good meals and the cutting of the *Vassilópitta*. This relative of the pound cake also conceals a coin that brings good fortune to the finder.

The feasting finally comes to an end on Epiphany and January 7th, St. John's day. Then a brief recovery period precedes Carnival, which usually begins around the end of January.

CARNIVAL AND LENT

The next three weeks of increasingly frenetic revelry are paralleled by the dedicated devouring of fabulous quantities of meat and cheese. The first week of Carnival is called *Gourounovdomáda* or Pig Week, the second *Arnovadomáda*, Lamb Week, and the final one *tis*

Tyrinús, Cheese Week. On the Sunday before Lent (called *Povero Carnavale*), the menu consists of macaroni with butter and cheese, followed by fried cheese and eggs *yia ti stríngla*, to ward off the evil eye. (You might have thought such an indigestible combination would bring it on.) The supper table is not cleared until morning in case any friendly spirits want to nibble during the night.

In some rural areas Carnival celebrations retained aspects of the fertility rites they once were, harking back to Dionysiac revels and even earlier. But while the country people wore goat-skin masks and humongous strapped-on phalluses, the Ionian townspeople replaced these with more elegant Venetian disguises. The new costumes also gave women the liberty to join in the fun without fear of recognition. Nicknamed *maskaroúles*, the ladies would completely conceal themselves in domino outfits and, communicating only through squeaks and gestures, tease the men outrageously. The British took a dim view of Carnival, limiting it to only two weeks in an attempt to clamp down on debauchery. Carnival traditionally was also a time for satirical plays and skits mocking the establishment, including inept physicians, corrupt lawyers and judges, and rich, warty-chinned widows. Such plays are still staged in Zakynthos.

Kathari Devtéra, Clean Monday, rather than Ash Wednesday, marks the beginning of Lent. Far from being a solemn occasion, it is rather a day dedicated to elaborate picnics of the most delectable fasting foods. Here the traditional tidbits are panhellenic, enjoyed from the Ionian as far east as Thrace, as far south as Kastellorizo. Usually present are sweet oysters and clams, delicate crayfish, stewed or pickled octopus, fluffy *taramosaláta*, crisp romaine lettuce leaves and spring onions, fiery pickles, pureed *fáva* (split yellow peas), lentil or potato salad, and, most of all, the platter-sized loaves of fresh baked *lagána*, the unleavened bread eaten only on this day. Inordinate quantities of wine are consumed, as if to ease the transition into Lent. This banquet, where no meat, eggs, cheese, or butter are present, ushers in forty days of fasting, which until the past few decades almost all Greeks observed. In the past, housewives would spend the morning scrubbing all the tables, cupboards, platters, and pans that had come into contact with meat, perhaps giving the day its name.

Even as late as the early 1970s fasting was so widespread that it was nearly impossible to find any meat served in country tavernas during the weeks before Easter. In addition to anything with blood, the faithful renounce dairy products and eggs, and housewives store their hens' eggs to dye them red for Easter. Although fish are taboo, shellfish, which we consider such a luxury, are consumed without compunction. Only on Wednesdays and Fridays are people meant to forgo olive oil—the ultimate hardship—and during Holy Week meals are more meager still, consisting largely of olives, *halváh* (loaves of sesame-seed paste sweetened with honey), and bitter greens or pulses cooked without olive oil. On Good Friday, a pious housewife will not even set the table, much less cook. Hanging the laundry or hammering a nail are also anathema, reminders of Christ's sufferings. Even nowadays some tavernas serve only permitted foods at this time, while the fishmongers close down altogether. The butchers stay open, their shops nearly invisible behind curtains of slaughtered kids and lambs hanging in wait for the Easter feast. But for most younger Greeks today, fasting is outmoded, and hamburgers, pizza, and souvlaki have taken its place.

Besides the forty-day Easter and Christmas fasts, the Greek religious calendar also prescribes shorter fasts before Assumption Day on the 15th of August and the Finding of the True Cross on September 14th. Health experts now testify to the benefits of giving one's system a rest, but in the winter, at least in the days before refrigeration when some foods were scarce, fasting was also a good way of economizing, while at the same time providing an antidote to holiday excesses.

Strangely, Greek fasting dishes bear no puritan traces. This is not food to induce piety or a sense of deprivation. Instead, rich with olive oil and seasonings, they are gratifying concoctions that are welcome the year round. Nevertheless, the old rhythm of feasting and fasting provided a balance that we with our nonstop feasting lack.

EASTER

Easter is the greatest holiday in the Orthodox Church. In most of the country, it is celebrated according to a prescribed set of rituals, beginning with the Good Friday funeral processions, peaking with the Resurrection service at midnight on Saturday, and relaxing into a bucolic lamb-roasting party the next day. The Ionian Islands, particularly Zakynthos and Corfu, do things somewhat differently, often to the beat of a marching band.

If everyone loves a parade, nobody loves one more than the denizens of these islands. While the rest of Greece waits for dusk to fall before joining their congregation's solemn course through town or village in a reenactment of Christ's entombment, the Corfiots and Zakynthians commemorate His crucifixion in the early afternoon. They wind through the streets behind a large crucifix and come to a halt precisely at 3:00 P.M., the hour that Christ died.

In Corfu, the *epitáphios* or funeral procession starts a few hours later. Though it is still light, everyone carries a beeswax candle and talks in whispers. One after another, the brass bands—there are said to be seventeen on the island—set the mournful pace, playing Chopin's *Marche Funebre*, the dead march from Handel's *Saul*, and Franco Faccio's funeral march from *Amletto*. All evening the bands pass through town in full regalia, led by brocaded priests behind the flowered bier.

In Zakynthos, however, the *epitáphios* procession from the Cathedral, does not take place until four o'clock the next morning, all the more doleful in the predawn chill. The candles flicker along the arcades like a massive stream of fireflies. Meanwhile, in a lighter vein, young men are plotting pranks more typical of Carnival. A few hours later, they'll be switching street and shop signs, painting new, risqué spellings over innocent names, and generally wreaking havoc.

Holy Saturday is a time for still more parading. In Corfu, a procession in honor of one of St. Spýridon's miracles starts off the morning. As soon as this is over (at eleven o'clock), the population is poised for the First Resurrection (*Próti Anástasi*), which the Zakynthians have celebrated four hours earlier. Despite the time difference, the residents of the main towns of these two islands share a custom found nowhere else in Greece. They pick this moment to hurl their old plates, jugs, and other crockery from their windows onto the street below, while the churchbells erupt into an ear-rupturing frenzy exacerbated by a tirade of firecrackers. This behavior has its roots in Psalm 2, verse 9: "Thou shalt dash them [the heathen] in pieces like a potter's vessel." The islanders call it "casting out Judas."

After this, the Corfiot bands come out once more, with joyful music and, instead of priests, two groups of *mazorétes* or majorettes, local high school girls whirling pompoms as if they were at an American college football game. A wagon piled high with red Easter eggs follows in their prancing steps, escorted by a couple of musicians playing a violin and a mandolin. The eggs are distributed to the crowd, which disperses until the next great gathering, around midnight.

The rest of the day passes quietly, though in Corfu up until a short while ago, residents used to slaughter the Easter lambs on Holy Saturday right in the middle of town. Rivulets of blood would flow through the streets, and in a curious custom reminiscent of Passover, each doorway would be emblazoned with a bloody cross.

Midnight on Saturday is a magical moment on all the islands and in Greece generally. The churches are packed, the squares outside them brimming with expectant latecomers, each one clutching an unlit candle. At the first stroke the priest emerges from the darkened church with a lit candle and proclaims the eagerly awaited words, "*Christós anésti*" (Christ is risen). As the flame moves from the bishop's taper through the congregation's candles, the bands blare forth, rockets flash, firecrackers explode, and the church bells all over town peal exultantly. A few of the faithful try (in vain) to sing the wonderful Easter hymn against the commotion.

In Corfu and Zakynthos town, there is a display of fireworks before the crowds disperse. But everywhere else, each family leaves the scene quickly, hoping to return home with at least one candle still burning. Once safely there, the father will make a smudgy cross on the lintel of the front door to protect the household for the year.

Only then may the fast legitimately be broken, though many Ionians consider that celebrating the First Resurrection gives them license to nibble on liver or chops with impunity earlier in the day. Traditionally, the midnight meal consists of red eggs, feta cheese, and *mageirítsa*, a rich egg-lemon soup made of lamb innards, spring onions, and dill. The Corfiot and Zakynthos versions, *tsilíkourda* and *tzaghétto*, are more like stew than soup and contain slightly different ingredients—tomatoes may even replace the eggs and lemon in *tsilíkourda*.

The lamb itself is eaten the following noon, but not, in Corfu at any rate, before another magnificent procession has taken place, this time lead by an icon of Christ.

Traditions also govern the preparation of the Easter lamb, but for the most part these are similar throughout Greece, with some minor variations. The Zakynthians, for example, roast their lambs on vine twigs in the oven. Usually the men of each clan are responsible for the cooking: they skewer the lamb and sew up its belly, often stuffing it with thyme sprigs and a halved lemon or two; they dig the

Procession of St. Spýridon, with sick parishioners lying in the road so the holy bier will pass over them

barbecue pit in the courtyard, fill it with charcoal, and heroically rise to light it just a few hours after the midnight meal has ended. By nine or ten o'clock one man will be turning the lamb slowly, while a squad of others offers helpful remarks, discusses soccer team scores, or makes baleful predictions about the weather, before settling in for their pastime, bashing the government. From time to time a woman will dart from the kitchen with a plate of bread and cheese, refilling coffee cups until the men decide to shift to wine, ouzo, or beer (usually no later than eleven). The men take turns rotating the lamb, and someone bastes it now and then with a brush made of more thyme sprigs, dipped into a bowl of salt, peppered olive oil, and lemon juice. In the course of the morning neighbors drop in and out, red eggs are cracked, *taramosaláta* and *tzatzíki* (yogurt mixed with garlic and cucumber) are sampled, glasses are emptied and reemptied until the lamb, skin crackling, juices streaming, aromas painfully tempting, is taken off the spit. The greedier guests take swipes at the crispy skin; the more patient wait for their plates to be piled with chunks of tender meat. Roast potatoes are produced, a lettuce leaf or a radish, but today the lamb is all anyone is really interested in. The eating is a lengthy process, mouthfuls savored, plates sent back for seconds, more wine to wash it down until, finally sated, the party slumps into semitorpor. But not for long. Sugar is needed to replenish energies, and sugar is forthcoming. Disks of honey-drenched oriental pastries circulate—*baklavás, galaktoboúreko, kataífi*—and then someone puts on a record or reaches for an instrument. As the fiddles whine and the mandolin tinkles, bodies jerk awake, feet tap the ground, and first one then another young man or woman rises to dance. Once the dancing starts, the party can go on forever, or at least well into the night. In Zakynthos, for instance, the fireworks and *panigýria* continue for seven nights after Easter.

SUMMER HOLIDAYS

Apart from such pastoral holidays as the first of May and Whitmonday (the British holiday that falls the day after Pentecost), spring and summer have fewer major celebrations than the other two seasons. The most important event during this period is the feast of the Assumption of the Virgin on August 15th. With so many Greeks and Ionians named Maria or Panayiótis (from the word for the Virgin Mary, *Panayía* or "all holy"), this is an important name day. Birthdays are a recent Western import; children and adults alike— almost everyone being named after a saint—celebrate their name days instead with a party, favorite meal, or open house. And because every other church seems to be dedicated to the Virgin, there are *panigýria* everywhere. With more rituals commemorating the finding of the True Cross on September 14th (see page 196), plus several autumnal processions in honor of the three main patron saints, it is no wonder the English were awestruck by the Ionians' "excessive fondness for amusement and display." All agreed, nonetheless, that "there never was a people with such a capacity for enjoyment."

WEDDINGS

This passion for enjoyment has traditionally been greatly in evidence before and during a wedding, where festivities could last up to a week. In Ithaca, for example, on the Thursday before the event, all the guests would arrive at the couple's home to prepare the nuptial bed, bearing presents and a packet of cotton. After stuffing the mattress with lambs' wool and the pillows with the cotton, the unmarried girls would sew up the mattress with a long thread and needle, although only those with both parents alive were allowed to participate. While they were making the bed, they would bounce a baby boy up and down with the sheet as if his presence would augur male children. Once the bed was dressed, a girl would lay a tray of sugared almonds on it and all the guests would file through the room, taking a handful of almonds and throwing money in their place. Then someone would smash a pomegranate against the door to elicit prosperity and fertility.

After the ceremony itself, on the following Sunday, a huge feast awaited the guests, a whole calf cut up and boiled in three or four huge cauldrons, followed by a lamb or kid roast on the spit. A father often set aside a thousand-kilo barrel of wine for his daughter's wedding. Here is Private Wheeler's impression of one such wedding menu:

"Dinner was served up in a large brass kettle round which the party . . . formed a circle, each armed with a formidable spoon. The contents of the kettle consisted of a goat stewed to rags, well thickened with rice and highly seasoned with pepper and garlic. After demolishing this, a sheep, roasted on a wooden spit, was brought in. . . . Each person now changed his fork for a knife." He went on to describe the dancing and carousing that lasted round the clock. Matters became more serious when the bride crossed the threshold of her new home: her mother-in-law would be waiting to feed her a spoonful of sugar to make her character sweet and docile. The bride must have wished for a potion with which to charm her new relative; not so long ago, in Corfu at any rate, once she became engaged she would have had to spend all her daytime hours doing chores for her prospective husband's very demanding family.

EVERYDAY LIFE BEFORE THE SECOND WORLD WAR

Even on nonfeast days, walking through the flagstone alleys of the Ionian towns into the wider streets flanked by arcades must have seemed festive. Not only did their shops compare with the best in Europe, both in merchandise and style, but the Anatolian spirit of doing business combined with their overall western character embued them with a unique vivacity.

In Corfu, as Tsitsas writes, the polyglot cries of the shoeshine boys and shopkeepers would mingle with the shouts of the peripatetic vendors. "*Calðe le patate*" went up the call for piping hot sweet and ordinary potatoes swathed in linen to keep the heat; "*Kástana marónia*," roast chestnuts still warming on the edge of the brazier; "*misóvolo kai voúta*," half a penny to dunk your bread into a huge pan of tripe soup. The same shop also offered portions of roast or boiled pork to take home. Depending on the season, you could get grilled artichokes, so young their "choke" was edible or, during Lent, boiled broad beans, sprinkled with salt and oregano in a cornet for immediate consumption or with their broth in a little pot if you were too busy or too poor to have cooked lunch. Another stand would have trimmed radishes and

Fishmonger

large bunches of pungent arugula, still another prickly pears, peeled for each customer, oozing their saccharin juices down the vendor's arm.

There were so many wonderful things simmering in the center of town that Lawrence Durrell baptized one corner "the street of smells." Here you could find sardines, shrimp, and cuttlefish, fresh and crunchy from the deep frier (only one shop still sells these — pans of them sit temptingly on a small counter not far from the jewelry and fur boutiques meant to attract the tourists); containers dripping with pickled octopus (sold by the forkful); and barrels of *savoúro* or marinated fish. During Lent, fish would be absent from the market, replaced by bloodless oysters, clams, mussels, squid, spiny sea urchins, and other fruits of the sea. A few doors down (except during Lent), the butchers made a kind of blood sausage — stuffed into its casing with salt, pepper, and onion, then sizzled in oil and vinegar with more onion — whose tempting odors only the very strong-minded could resist. In winter, the charcoal fires and acetylene lights of the vendors cheered up the sodden streets, while the red flags waving from the tavernas proclaimed the arrival of the new wine, another item to gladden a dreary winter evening. Until well after the war Ionian tavernas served no food. Drinking parties would bring their own *mezédes*, a little herring, bread, or olives, for no Greek would touch alcohol without eating something with it.

In Zakynthos, too, before the earthquake practically every other shop represented the Ionian version of "fast food." Many of them catered to workers, offering a meal for a few *lépta* or pennies. Here they could choose from among several capacious pans containing plaited innards (*gardoúmba*), stewed liver, stuffed spleen, or *pancetta* (more like spare ribs than bacon), all steeped in bubbling, fragrant juices. As soon as the proprietor appeared in his doorway with a shout that the food was ready, the laborers would stop work, pick up a loaf of bread from the baker, and line up outside the shop for the *voúta*, or "dipping." Five *lépta* would buy them the chance to soak their bread, broken into bite-sized chunks, in the broth, ten would grant them access to the more succulent corners where the oil and fat had collected. They could consume their gravy-soaked loaves at simple tables on the spot or wrap them in wax paper together with a piece of the meat and take them to a nearby taverna. There, with a tumbler or two of wine and some congenial company, the humble meal would turn into a party and *cantádes* or ballads would fill the air as soon as it was eaten. One taverna in Zakynthos continues this tradition even today. Once a week it serves bits of roast lamb, offal, and other meats free to its regular customers and anyone else who happens to drop in for the *voúta*.

Lefkada, being more Anatolian, used to have whole streets resembling Asian bazaars with merchandise spilling out into the sidewalks or hanging in bunches like garish Christmas ornaments on the shopfront. Their rice, beans, pasta, and olives invited inspection from well-used barrels or sacks instead of today's pre-measured hygienic packets. Martin Young in his wonderful guide to the Ionian says that no other main street in the Ionian was "so bursting with food and drink and wares of every kind." Until recent years, few of its shops had stylish show windows and the workmen still stopped to slurp *patsás* (tripe soup) in small murky cookeries that rarely entertained a tourist. Out in the sunlight country women still sail by in their voluminous long-sleeved dresses of brown, dark green, blue, or crimson satin.

Before the war the Ionians, being a gregarious, curious, theatrical people, conducted a good portion of their social lives on the street. Many of them might not have been able to afford to invite guests to their home more often than the name-day open house, but with their morning shopping and their evening promenades they made certain that nothing of any significance escaped them.

In all the main towns, however, women from good families were rarely seen on the street by day. In Zakynthos, in the last century, if they had to deal with laborers on their estates, they would conceal their face behind a Zorro mask. Their place was in the home, where if they were rich enough they had country people to work for them. Women spent their mornings supervising the cooking or cleaning, filling any leisure hours with embroidering, reading French and German novels in the original, or practicing the piano. They received callers or gossiped with their next-door neighbors over the balcony railing. On no account did they go to market; shopping was the province of the husband or sons. Even a widow or spinster would have had some male relative to bring her groceries. This custom was not without its complications, for husbands would often shop for their mistresses at the same time, employing a porter armed with two large baskets instead of one. Corfiots still tell the story of the porter who got the baskets mixed up and the wife received the lobster, wild strawberries, and other delicacies intended for her rival.

Every household that could afford it had a young village girl of between eleven and fourteen to clean the furniture, lay the table, and polish the silver. She generally did not have her own room and often her bed was just a linen chest covered with a sheet and blanket. Nor was she paid. But she did attend school and grew up well versed in the arts of housekeeping. Her employers often provided her with a dowry and a fine wedding.

As for the cooking, it was often done on the *foufoú*, a ceramic charcoal brazier, which doubled as a heater. Most houses in Cephalonia, Ithaca, and Zakynthos, urban and rural alike, also possessed a portable clay oven, which many women still prefer to their electric ranges. Called a *tserépa*, it consists of an earthenware or, today, a metal cover that is placed on top of a baking tin and then sealed with dough. The oven is set among red-hot coals, surrounded with ashes and left until the contents have cooked to perfection. This was and is a favorite way to make traditional meat or vegetable pies, roast chicken, or meat and potatoes. Even the Easter lamb was cut up and baked in the tserépa until the skewer ritual gradually replaced it a couple of decades ago.

RURAL LIFE

The life of the peasants in the Ionian differed radically from that of the city dwellers. One could almost say that they belonged to another country, which had barely changed from the days of the Romans to the fall of Venice. Only when the British abolished feudalism did their lot begin to improve.

While the townspeople had mingled with the foreigners, adopted their language, their customs, their fashions, and, to some extent, their cuisine, their rural cousins spoke only Greek, farmed the way their ancestors had, dressed in their traditional costumes, and ate extremely simply. Their kitchens were primitive, no copper saucepans or laminated ovens here—and sometimes their kitchens were not even inside the house. In Lefkada in 1863, for example, a Professor Ansted reported visiting a kitchen that was "separated from the house by a little paved passage. It is a large shed, but with no other apertures than the door and a hole in the roof to let out smoke and let in light. The hearth is a large space raised about four inches from the floor and serves not only to hold the sticks that made the fire, but as the place where all kinds of scullery work are carried out by boys, or girls, squatted down beside it. . . . The kitchen utensils are limited to the smallest possible number, and do not include a pair of tongs, or more than one spoon and fork for cooking purposes."

A few kitchens matching this description are still in use in Zakynthos and elsewhere, their walls completely blackened with soot.

On winter nights, rural families always ate their soup or boiled greens sitting on the floor around the fire. In fact, the poorest households had no furniture except for a chest and beds. Their bedding, however, could be very luxurious, piled high with lovely linen, embroideries, and blankets; these were the only items creditors were not permitted to impound.

In the Corfiot village of Synarádes, there is a small folk museum in a three-story building that has been kept the way it was from 1860 to 1960, when it provided living quarters for two comparatively well-off families above the stable, the oven, and the storeroom where firewood, wine, charcoal, and oil were kept. The kitchen has no stove, only an open fireplace where a cauldron rests on a tripod. If the fire were blazing it could be raised to different levels with a chain connected to a hook in the chimney. A few other blackened pots, ladles, and spoons hang on the wall next to it. Against the wall opposite are a wooden trough for kneading dough, a large square chest in which dry foods—beans, flour, rice, bread—were stored, a

Traditional cooking fireplace

few shelves with assorted platters and dishes. Suspended from the ceiling, the *fanári*, a screened cabinet for perishables, let air circulate but kept out flies and mice. There was no running water. A two-gallon metal container with a little spigot hangs from the wall above a rudimentary stone sink. A straight-backed wooden chair and a simple bench provided stiff seating facing the fire. The glazed ochre jar containing olive oil is too large for the kitchen; it stands in the tiny entrance hall.

Each family slept in a single bedroom, where the dowry trunk still displays neatly piled bedspreads and sheets, unyellowed by the passing years. Chamberpots are tucked discreetly under the beds. There was no plumbing, but there was a vegetable garden below. The women would have carried water jugs on their heads from the town well or spring and washed their heavier laundry in the sea some hours walk away.

The country people of all the islands subsisted on wild greens, pulses, fruit, local cheeses, olives, cornbread, and olive oil. They often grew their own vegetables; artichokes and members of the cabbage and onion families were the most common. They also raised chickens but took the eggs to market and ate them only on special occasions or when someone was ill and needed a fortifying broth. Although gathering the greens was a necessity, the women seemed to go about it cheerfully—singing as they dug, cleaned, and trimmed the weeds. Of course, they knew all about the plants: which were sweet, which bitter, and which were good for ailments. They picked chamomile for colic, chicory to thin the blood, onion as a diuretic, garlic for worms. In the absence of doctors, herbs and natural remedies were all a woman had to treat her family. Curiously, picking *hórta* (greens) is still a popular pastime. None of the prejudices associated with hard times seem to have dimmed people's pleasure in selecting and eating them; cornbread, on the other hand, is another matter, and it rarely appears on the table.

So many varieties of greens exist and there are so many different names for them that it would be folly to try to translate them all. But apart from the more typical dandelions, sorrel, wild chicory, purslane, and wild bulbs, the islanders also pick samphire (*Crithmum maritimum*) from the cliffs near the shore; they call it *kritamón* and pickle it for future eating with *skordaliá* (garlic sauce). The quest for capers also takes them to the cliffs, while some of the rocks under the water yield an edible seaweed.

The peasants in the mountains, always poorer than the people who lived in the lowlands and near the ports, sometimes supplemented their diet with currants. One such Zakynthos dish, called *mammí* or *mammítsa*, consisted simply of some sliced onion sauteed in oil, to which a handful of wheat flour was added, then browned and topped off with a sprinkling of currants. *Lípsa* was even more rudimentary: a batter of flour, salt, and water fried in olive oil and served with a sugar syrup, if they were lucky enough to have a bit of sugar. But, generally, honey gathered from their own bees was the universal sweetener.

Though shepherds' and farmers' households on the mainland often made their own pasta, the practice was not as widespread in the Ionian. Thin noodles called *toumátsi* and *trífta roliá* (pasta grated into small pieces) were a Cephalonian specialty, while *trachaná*, sour milk mixed with flour and salt and dried in the sun, was most commonly found in Cephalonia, Ithaca, and Lefkada.

There is no question that life was hard for the country people on the islands. But it was not lonely. The extended family brought up the children; women picked *hórta*, washed blankets, and worked the fields together; men gathered around a friend's wine barrel to tell stories. In Zakynthos, there was even an institution—the *gaidarotavérna* or "donkey tavern"—on the main routes to town, where farmers would stop on their way back from market. Even so, one can well understand why so many *panigýria* were needed to break the routine.

PREPARING THE KITCHEN

PROSPERO'S LARDER: NOTES ON THE INGREDIENTS

Described below are some of the ingredients used in the recipes that every Ionian cook would have at her elbow but which might not be familiar to you.

CHEESES / *TYRIÁ*

Ionian cheeses are not notably different from those in the rest of Greece, though some Swiss friends of ours maintain that Corfu *graviéra* tastes more like the original Gruyère than any other (almost every region in Greece has a *graviéra*). Corfu also makes a local version of Parmesan but it cannot be compared to the one from Parma.

The most common cheeses are the ubiquitous feta, made from ewe's or cow's milk, and *myzíthra*, which is akin to Italian *ricotta* when fresh. It is used for grating after it has hardened into a solid white ball about the size of an ostrich egg.

Kefalotýri is a popular, sharp, hard cheese used widely for grating. Greek friends living in America tell us that Romano is the substitute for it.

Perhaps the most original cheeses are from Zakynthos. One called *Prétza* is like a crumbly feta; flavored with thyme sprigs, it has a peppery taste. The other, *ladotýri*, takes its name (oil cheese) from the practice of aging it in barrels of olive oil. It is a crumbly, piquant cheese, with a taste comparable to pecorino but with a softer consistency. When fresh, it has a creamy taste and texture.

Fyllo or Strudel Pastry

1. Most large supermarkets have 1 pound packets of *fyllo* (often called strudel pastry) in their freezers. Before you intend to use it, remove it from your refrigerator and let it reach room temperature. If you try to work with it cold, you'll find it brittle.

2. There are generally twelve sheets of pastry in a 1 pound (½ kilo) packet. Half is used for the bottom of a pie and half for the top.

3. Each sheet of pastry should be brushed with melted butter, margarine, or olive oil according to the specific recipe.

4. Cover the remaining leaves with a damp cloth while you are working or they will dry out.

5. Score the pie in square or diamond shapes before baking.

6. Sprinkle the top of the pie with a little water before baking to prevent the pastry from splitting.

Garlic / *Skórdo*

You will note that some of these recipes call for large quantities of garlic. But remember that cooked garlic becomes sweet and loses its offensiveness. To make it more "socially correct" when using it raw, remove the green shoot in each clove, if there is one. Garlic also differs in pungency depending on type. Small but strong, Cephalonian garlic has a mauve tinge; Zakynthian giant garlic is white and less dynamic.

HERBS / *VÓTANA*

As a general rule, fresh herbs are always preferable to dried ones. Most herbs, such as rosemary, mint, thyme, and oregano, dry well, but basil loses all its taste when dried. When using dried herbs, halve the amount suggested for fresh.

Basil / *Vasilikós*

The royal herb (*vasileús* means king) is little used in mainland cooking, but the Ionians add it to their stuffed and baked vegetable dishes. It marries especially well with tomatoes. Helen, the mother of Constantine, the first Christian emperor, found a large patch of basil growing in Jerusalem where the Cross was said to have stood. Greek priests bless houses and boats with a bunch of it sprinkled with holy water. No Ionian house would be without a pot of this fragrant herb on its balcony or terrace.

Bay Leaves / *Dáfni*

Named after a nymph who changed into a laurel tree to escape Apollo's advances, these leaves are indispensable in stews and marinades. Dried, they are just as good as fresh.

Celery / *Sélino*

Greek celery is dark green with slender stalks and a profusion of leaves. It looks very similar to the so-called Italian or flat-leaved parsley, but the taste is unmistakable. It is, however, much more flavorful than the Pascal celery commonly sold in the United States. Use celery leaves and tips in these Ionian dishes.

Dill / *Ánitho*

This feathery herb goes well with artichoke, pea, and broad bean stews. It almost always adorns a romaine lettuce salad and is the main seasoning in Easter soup. It was so valuable to the ancient Romans they even put a tax on it.

Fennel / *Máratho*

This anise-flavored herb grows wild all over the Greek countryside. Use the leaves or a bit of fennel bulb as a substitute. Its taste is much stronger than the domestic variety, so you can use more of that than what's suggested if it appeals to you.

Marjoram / *Madzourána*
Sweeter than oregano, this is a key seasoning in Cephalonian pie.

Mint / *Dyósmos*
Spearmint, used abundantly in the Ionian, perks up vegetable dishes, meat balls, and meat pies.

Oregano / *Rígani*
Another herb found all over Ionian hillsides, it is most often used dried, even in Greece. It is closely related to marjoram but has a sharper taste. Dishes with feta, stuffings, and roast chicken profit from the addition of *rígani*.

Parsley / *Maindanó*
At the Nemean Games in antiquity the winners were awarded wreaths of parsley. When we refer to parsley in these recipes, we always mean the flat-leaved, so-called Italian variety. The curly leaved kind may look nicer as a garnish, but it cannot compare in taste.

Rose Geranium / *Arbaróriza*
Their sweetly scented leaves are used in jams and spoonsweets and add an especially delicate flavor to quince and seedless grape preserves.

Rosemary / *Dendrolívano*
For remembrance; this herb's name in Greek means "tree incense." It has a strong aroma, so a few sprigs go a long way. Try grilling fish with a twig stuffed in its belly; or use it with roast pork or chicken. The Corfiots like a tablespoon of it tossed at the last minute in the frying pan with potatoes.

Honey / *Méli*
An ancient sweetener, beloved of the islanders. There are three main types of honey in Greece, their characters determined by what the bees have fed on: thyme, wildflowers, or conifers. Thyme honey from the mountains of Cephalonia, the Volimes area of Zakynthos,

and from Kythera is especially good. Besides being used in syrups to be poured over sweet pies and cakes, honey is wonderful with yogurt. It is of course much healthier for you than sugar, from which all the nutrients have been "refined."

Mavrodáphne Wine
A heavy, sweet wine that would be hard to serve with dinner but is wonderful to cook with.

Petimési
Grape must that is boiled down to a sweet syrup, this is called *vino cotto* in Italian and is stocked by some specialized grocery stores. We suggest using a sweet red wine like *Mavrodáphne* if you cannot find it.

Pine nuts / *Koukounária*
From the cones of the umbrella pine, these are more widely used in Greek dishes from Anatolia than in the Ionian. Because they are so expensive, keep them in the refrigerator. Stale, they would ruin your dish.

Pulses / *Óspria*
The whole family of dried beans and peas are staples of the Ionian diet. No cupboard would be complete without a choice of lentils, chick-peas (garbanzos), white beans, black-eyed peas, and split yellow peas. Confusingly, these are called *fáva* in Greek and should not be mistaken for Italian fava beans, which are actually broad beans. Black beans and split green peas are not part of the Greek diet. If your pulses never soften after hours of boiling, your water may be too hard. Try cooking them with rain water or, failing that, bottled water, adding salt after cooking.

Rice / *Rísi*
There are at least five types of rice available in Greek markets, but the most commonly used are short grain rice for soups and vegetable stuffings and long grain for pilaffs.

Rusks / *Paximádia*

Many of the recipes in this book call for rusk crumbs. Usually we mean thick slices of twice-baked peasant bread, crumbled.

Rusks are very popular in Greece and come in all kinds of varieties. Some are sweet, containing spices such as aniseed or cinnamon, like the Zakynthos rusks on page 203, or currants. Others are plain, like the Kytheran ones on page 204. They are usually so hard you can hardly bite off a chunk. The Greeks like to soften them in their coffee or tea. Left to soak up olive oil and vinegar or even wine, rusks also make delicious, informal snacks (see Appetizers).

They can replace a pie crust, add a crunchy topping to a baked fish, or even substitute for cheese.

They are also easy to make at home with leftover country bread. Just cut slices about ½-inch thick and bake them in a very low oven (250° F. / 120° C.) until golden and dry. Turn them every now and then so both sides dry out equally (at least 1 hour). Cool in the oven and store in a tin. They will keep for months if you don't eat them. Some Venetian rusks lasted over a century with no harm done.

Toast crumbs could be substituted for rusks in these recipes.

Salt Cod / *Bakaliáro*

Who would have thought there was a secret to soaking salt cod? This tip from a yachtsman friend will reduce the time needed to leach out the salt.

First, hold the fish under the cold water tap to rinse off the salt clinging to the surface. Then fill a large bowl with cold water. If you have a piece of plastic or wire netting or a steamer rack, place that in the bowl and let the fish rest on it. The salt that permeates its flesh will sink to the bottom of the bowl, so if the fish is "suspended" above it, it will not reabsorb the salt. Soak the fish for about twenty-four hours, changing the water four times. Soaking without the net may take as long as thirty-six hours or even two days.

Sesame Seeds / *Sousámi*

Full of vitamins, these tiny seeds are sprinkled lavishly on Greek breads. They are also made into candy bars called *pastélli*.

Semolina / *Simigðáli*

The old breakfast cereal, cream of wheat, in a different guise is a common ingredient of Ionian cakes and puddings. It is made of durum wheat, the flour employed in pasta, and comes in three types: coarse, medium (cream of wheat consistency), and fine. While the first two are used in cakes and puddings, fine semolina is the flour that makes Greek and Sicilian bread distinctive.

SPICES / *BACHARIKÁ*

Allspice / *Bachári*

This relative of the myrtle berry seems to be a combination of all the familiar spices, hence its name in both Greek and English. It is not widely used except in some stews and game dishes.

Cayenne / *Kókkino Pipéri*

It seems that the Corfiots, alone among the Ionian islanders, have a hot tooth. They use cayenne pepper liberally in a series of fish and vegetable dishes called *bourðéttos*.

Cinnamon / *Kanélla*

A stick of cinnamon is a favorite addition to many stews, pasta sauces, and honey syrup. Powdered, it is sprinkled on doughnuts, cakes, and both sweet and savory pies. It has been prized since antiquity. Cinnamon is often found in combination with cloves (*garýfala*), which must be used sparingly. Whole cloves add flavor to soups, marinades, stuffings, and stews. Powdered, they harmonize well with Zakynthos ham, rabbit, and pumpkin, especially, as well as fasting cookies and cakes.

Nutmeg / *Moschokárydo*

Literally, "the aromatic nut," a little grated nutmeg goes into a béchamel sauce or some spice cakes.

Paprika

Although much beloved in most Balkan countries, only the Corfiots seem to use it.

Taramás

Once this was mashed grey mullet roe; now it comes from cod. Try to buy *taramá* paste that is pinkish-grey rather than Day-Glo pink. The latter will probably be terribly salty. The best brands come from Scandinavia, Russia, and Iceland and are sold by weight or in small vacuum sealed bags.

Tomatoes / *Domátes*

Everyone knows what a tomato is, or thinks they do. Tomatoes in Greece still taste the way they're supposed to, at least from June through October. Nowadays the Greeks eat tomatoes from greenhouses in the winter, but they can't compare to the red, sweet, sun- and vine-ripened variety. If your tomatoes are pale and watery, use canned tomatoes instead or even tomato paste in preference. Or do as the Corfiots and add some sun-dried tomatoes to your stews and soups.

Many of these recipes call for grated tomatoes. Greek cooks seem to prefer grating to chopping them and we, too, have adopted this habit.

Yogurt / *Yiaoúrti*

The yogurt referred to in our recipes is much thicker than any yogurt available in the US. Almost all the water has been strained out of it. It gets its Greek name, *sakkoúlas*, from the cheesecloth bags in which ordinary yogurt is hung up to drain. You can achieve the same effect by taking plain yogurt and draining it through a sieve lined either with a couple of thicknesses of cheesecloth or a large coffee filter. Stir a tablespoonful of salt into the yogurt and keep it in the refrigerator or a cool place for twenty-four hours with a container placed underneath to catch the water. The salt will drain out along with the water. Remember that you'll have about half the amount of yogurt that you started out with.

Before the age of plastic, Greek yogurt, which is made from either cow's or ewe's milk, was sold in earthenware pots of various sizes (up to a kilo). Although you can still find this traditional yogurt, many other kinds are available as well, with fat content ranging from 0 to 10 percent, and in dozens of flavors. The old-fashioned kind is wonderful topped with preserves or honey and walnuts. We in Greece use strained yogurt for American and other recipes that call for sour cream, which is not available here.

THE OLIVE TREE,
ITS OIL AND FRUIT

Even before Athena dueled with Poseidon over whose gift to man was more valuable—the olive tree or the horse, the tree was an inseparable part of Greek culture and civilization. Not only have olives and olive oil been a staple food for at least four millennia, the oil has also had an important role in religious practices, both pagan and Christian, along with the two other basics, bread and wine. In Homer's day, scented oils infused with wild rose petals, sage, mint, coriander, or cumin were used to anoint the body after bathing. Later, in lieu of soap, which had yet to be invented, athletes rubbed olive oil over their skin before and after training and competitions, then scraped it off along with any dirt. The winners and runners-up—at the Panathenaic Games at least—brought home not only olive wreaths but also special commemorative amphoras holding about 40 kilos of oil. A sprinter was awarded up to 2½ tons of the precious liquid, the best charioteer 5 tons!

Nowadays, Greeks consume more olive oil—21.5 quarts (or 20 liters) per person annually—than any other nationality. The country's 120 million trees represent 80 percent of its total tree cultivation, giving employment to hundreds of thousands of families and migrant

workers. Greece is also the biggest exporter of unbottled extra virgin olive oil, though it ranks third in total world production, after
Italy and Spain. About 700 tons of it end up in the United States.

THE CORFIOT OLIVE TREES

But if the olive tree is central to life in Greece, for centuries it was
absolutely vital to the existence of the Ionian islanders, especially the
Corfiots and the Paxiots. The peasants would have starved to death
without it, while the upper classes used oil in the place of cash,
stocks, and bonds. It was every bit as important to them as another
sort of oil is to Texans. For most Corfiots and Paxiots their trees
were their only source of income. All the islands have olive trees,
great numbers of them, but the Zakynthians also had their currants,
the Cephalonians and Ithacans their ships, and the Lefkadans and
Kytherans other crops to rely on.

The Corfiot trees are quite different from those in the rest of
Greece. They belong to the Lianolia variety, which the Venetians
brought from Italy to supplement the native stock. Because they are
rarely pruned, they are taller, wilder, and more mysterious, with
dark, sinewy trunks pitted with strange whorls and holes, their leafy
branches arching and meshing with those of their neighbors to
make a shaded forest impenetrable by the sun. In contrast, the
typical Peloponnesian olive trees (called *Koronéikes* from Koroni)
seem to grow out rather than up: stout trunks knotted and twisted,
extraneous branches lopped off, and the rest trained to droop
gracefully towards the ground to facilitate collection. Viewed from
above, Corfu's inland sea of silvery foliage quivers and shimmers
with the slightest breeze, interrupted here and there by clusters of
green-black cypress spires and the pale ochre rooftops of distant
villages. Viewed from alongside, the groves could set the stage for a
fairy tale; all kinds of imaginary spectral beings might lurk in their
mossy shadows.

Because their trees grow so immense, the Corfiots do not attempt
to knock the branches with long poles to get the fruit to drop off,
which has been the practice in the rest of Greece since antiquity.

Old olive grove

Boasting that they beat neither their wives nor their trees, they wait for the olives to ripen and fall of their own accord. As John Davy wrote in the 1830s, this is now a tradition and upheld almost as a virtue, or at least a necessary idiosyncrasy that evolved in response to the growing pattern of the tree. It means that rather than lasting a couple of months, the olive harvest extends from November to June, each tree being visited once a month.

Inevitably, this has given rise to endless disparaging remarks about the Corfiot character. Victorian gentlemen like Henry Jervis-White Jervis, an artillery officer stationed on the island in the early 1850s, never missed an opportunity to pass judgment: "Like the Greek of old, the Corfiot peasant loves to lounge away his time in the market place catering for every trifling piece of news. Indolent beyond belief, he is satisfied with the food that Providence affords him off the neighboring olive tree; which he patiently waits to see drop onto the ground."

NUTRITION AND HEALTH

He also remarked on the benefits of this marvellous tree. "The kindly berry (the free use of oil is said to correct the astringency of the wine and protect the stomach from its consequent effects), added to a piece of bread and some salt fish, forms his daily sustenance; its oil gives him light, and its wood supplies his fuel." But though the nutritional value of olive oil has long been known, Jervis would no doubt have been surprised to hear of all the almost miraculous properties that scientists have discovered in the past couple of decades. As for the Greeks, they have long considered olive oil not only a health-giving tonic but also an aphrodisiac. In the Ionian and elsewhere, you often hear the old saying, spoken with a bit of a leer, "*Fáei ládi ki' ela vrádi.*" (Eat some oil and come round in the evening.)

While doctors may be reluctant to emphasize this latter attribute, both pediatricians and geriatricians recommend that their patients eat olive oil with their food every day. Not only does it play a significant role in balancing the metabolism and developing young brains and bones, but its high vitamin E content makes it a natural antioxidant, acting against the free radicals that destroy cell membranes and hasten the aging process. It also helps to prevent ulcers by slowing down production of hydrochloric acid. It inhibits the formation of gallstones, and it helps reduce the negative effects of cholesterol, which is a leading cause of arteriosclerosis and heart disease.

Because it is a balanced synthesis of saturated and unsaturated fatty acids, it is crucial to a healthy diet. So don't wince when you see the suggested amounts of olive oil in some of the recipes included here. Bear in mind that these meals were cooked by and for people who led an active, often arduous life. That their diet was good for them is borne out by all the statistics showing longevity records in Greece. They also lived next to the source, so oil was cheap. We are aware of contemporary concerns about reducing fat intake and of the high price of olive oil outside the Mediterranean, so we have decreased recommended oil amounts in many cases. Still, if you wish to use even less oil, you can do so and the dish will remain tasty.

EXTRA VIRGIN, VIRGIN, AND PURE

Olive oil varies in quality depending on where it is grown — location, climate, weather, and soil conditions — and how it is produced. It is generally divided into three categories — extra virgin, virgin, and pure, according to acidity content, which should never be higher than 3.3 percent. Look for clarity, a fruity taste, and a fresh, not musty, smell. Extra virgin oil, which has a greenish hue, must have one percent oleic acid or lower; virgin 2 percent. Greece's finest olive oil, from the Kalamata region of the southern Peloponnese, is only 0.05 percent acid. The best oil is cold-pressed from underripe olives, which are processed as soon as possible after harvesting.

Acidity develops in olives if they are stored too long before pressing. This unfortunately means that the Corfiot practice of collecting olives once a month results in an oil closer to and sometimes even over the upper limit. In the old days, the women and children used to have to scramble, bent double, all over the uneven terrain to gather olives that had rolled under rocks or down slopes. The work was so gruelling — English aspersions to the contrary — that in the poverty-stricken decade after the Second World War many families abandoned their groves and sought employment in mainland industries.

THE OIL PRESS

Production methods had also remained primitive and time-consuming, little changed from Jervis's day when the oil was "manufactured by implements that would hardly be thought creditable to the age of the Phaeacians. A perpendicular stone wheel, revolving on a large horizontal stone of a circular form, and slightly hollowed in the center, is set in motion by a horse, and bruises the olives, which are shoveled in by a peasant. They are then placed in a mat bag and pressed by means of a clumsy screw; the oil oozing through the bag into a hole cut in the ground."

Hot water was poured over the bags to free the oil, which flowed into a barrel placed in the hole. After the oil rose to the surface, it was scooped into clean barrels and the water discarded. The whole process was so laborious it took five men and a horse to crush five hundred kilos of olives; today's machines can process eleven times as much oil in a single day.

The early 1960s brought the invention of the thickly woven black nylon net and the electric oil press, which have enticed some people back to the land and eased the lives of those that never left. Except in summer when they are rolled up and stuck neatly in the crooks of the trees, the nets blanket the floor of the groves, catching most of the crop. The acidity that accumulates in the olives that fall early in the month can be offset if they are cold pressed. In any case, the Corfiots are intensely proud of their golden oil and love its mild flavor. Ask a Zakynthian about it, however, and he will pucker his mouth in disapproval; Zakynthos oil is less than one percent acid.

OIL FOR MORE THAN EATING

Olive oil has many more uses than as a cooking medium or dressing for salads. Greek babies are christened with it; the lamps under the icons burn it. Desperate people during the war who were reduced to taking the oil from the church or face starvation made vows to build a new church using olive oil to mix the cement if they survived. Such churches are apt to be rather small.

Olive oil forms the basis for many home remedies and customs. For example, mixed with the yellow flowers of St. John's wort and left to stand in the sun all summer, it becomes a soothing balm for aches and pains that has been known since antiquity. Combined with half an onion and some grated soap, it forms an unusual but effective poultice. Painters pour a cupful into their whitewash to make it stick better, while a little oil sprinkled on the sea smooths it sufficiently for a fisherman to glimpse the unsuspecting octopus on the bottom. It is also the key ingredient for getting rid of the evil eye. When things tend to go badly with depressing regularity or you feel ill without being so, some envious acquaintance may have put the evil eye on you. Many Greek women, whether educated urbanites or unschooled farmer's wives, know how to remove the bane by pouring a couple of drops in a glass of water and muttering an incantation. If the oil disperses into bubbles instead of remaining amalgamated, the spell is lifted and life will resume its normal course. (Don't scoff. It works, at least some of the time.)

Needless to say, olive wood is also put to good use. Because a tree takes up to forty years to mature, both the ancient Athenians and the Venetians made it a crime to cut one down. But its trunk, larger branches and even roots make beautiful solid furniture, bowls, and utensils. Because the wood is so hard, it burns brightly but slowly, heating rooms that never knew central heating. Even olive pulp has its uses. Pressed cakes of it fuel many a rural oven and are an ingredient of some animal feeds.

THE KINDLY BERRY

Wild olives must have been among humanity's first foods during the hunting-gathering stage. Overripe olives eventually lose most of their bitterness without any treatment and are edible if not palatable. The wizened black olives called *throúmbes* belong to this category, though they are packed in salt for a few weeks to hasten the process and seasoned with *throúmbi*, a kind of marjoram, to add to their taste.

There are over sixty different kinds of olives; they fall into two categories, oil-producing and munchable. The two most popular varieties of eating olives in the Ionian and in Greece generally are the firm, tear-drop shaped Kalamata olives and the larger, softer, oval Amphissa olives.

The Lianolia olives of Corfu are much smaller, not more than 2 centimeters (less than an inch) long. Though they can be pickled and eaten, they are not found in the market but only in private homes.

Despite the great variety and sheer volume of olives consumed in the Ionian, there are very few recipes which call for olives to be cooked with the other ingredients rather than eaten raw as a garnish. We could only find a couple. Why this should be true is a mystery.

HOW TO PICKLE YOUR OWN OLIVES

Few Americans have access to uncured olives fresh from the tree, but just in case you come across them, here is how to render them edible. If they are ripe, slit each one with a sharp knife; if green, crack each one with a stone or hammer, taking care not to break the kernel. Then soak them in a large tub of water for 10 to 20 days, changing the water once a day, until there is no trace of bitterness. Next, prepare a brine solution using about a cup of salt for every quart of water. Place a whole raw egg in the water and add the salt gradually; Greek cooks say that the brine has just the right salinity when an egg will float in it. Keep the olives covered with brine in an airtight container stored in a cool, dark place.

If you prefer the tang of vinegar, you can soak them first in brine for 24 hours and then in vinegar for another 24 before storing them in a solution of oil and vinegar or just oil with any seasonings you choose.

Once any kind of olive is ready to eat, its flavor can be enhanced by adding herbs—thyme, oregano, fennel, garlic—and/or lemon slices and leaves to the oil and brine mixture in which they are stored. Do this to the ones you buy and experiment; you don't have to have cured the olives yourself.

THE WINES °F THE IONIAN

Be not misled. Not all Greek wines taste of resin. In fact, retsina was never drunk in the Ionian until the tourists, who had heard so much about this unique beverage, demanded that it be imported from the mainland. Instead, as might be expected, many Ionian wines have Italian sounding names, for along with the olive stock the Venetians brought in a variety of vines. For example, the Robola grapes used to make the islands' best known wine may have originally come from the slopes of Friuli northeast of Venice. Verdea, the wine of Zakynthos, may have taken its name from a medieval Tuscan wine with a similarly green tint.

In the past, visitors to the Ionian remarked on how ideally suited the landscape was to the cultivation of the vine. Its rocky soil, so full of the porous limestone that vines prefer, is ideal in combination with the spring rains and long hot summers. Vines had been growing there since Odysseus's time and probably long before. There are countless references in *The Odyssey* to both "ruby-colored" and "honey-hearted" wine and the hero's storeroom contained "jars of earthenware in rows, holding an old wine, mellow, unmixed and rare." Like the olive and its oil, grapes and wine are inseparable from Greek culture.

Wine processing, family-style

But wines have not always tasted the same. If Homer's audience preferred a sweet brew with a kick, so did many more recent generations. Wheler in the seventeenth century praised the red muscatels of Cephalonia, Murray's 1872 *Handbook* compared the Verdea of Zakynthos to the best Marsala, while Tertius Kendrick went even further: "The wines of Zante deserve highest praise, particularly the white, which so exactly resembles madeira that even a connoisseur might be deceived." He also found the Cephalonian wines so exquisite that he thought Englishmen might be inclined "to discontinue all French importations" if enough of them could taste it.

While Ionian wines had great potential, however, several factors also worked against them. Here, too, the Venetians can be held partially responsible. In Corfu, for example, they discouraged vine cultivation in favor of the olive. Even though they left the island two hundred years ago, some islanders still blame their relative lack of vineyards and wine-making expertise on the Venetians. On the southern islands, they appropriated extensive wine-growing estates for currant plantations. With England's seemingly insatiable demand for currants, the grape took second place to its far more lucrative cousin. Even today, two-thirds of Zante's vineyards are planted with this "black gold," rather than wine-producing grapes.

Old wine barrels

After unification with Greece, Ionian wine manufacturers also suffered from isolation, backward production methods, two major wars, and the Greek civil war. The 1953 earthquake coming so soon after the civil war crippled the wine industry still further. Several vineyards were destroyed and so many families left the islands that few people could be found to help restore them. Today, tourism is posing a new, double-edged threat. Prime land is being sold off for development and young people prefer well-paid seasonal employment in hotels and restaurants to working year-round in a possibly risky venture in the countryside. Nevertheless, many Ionian wines are worth drinking, and some—especially from Cephalonia and Zakynthos—are becoming available, and known, abroad.

ZAKYNTHOS

This island boasts the oldest wine-producing business in Greece. It was founded by a Count Comoútos in 1638 and has remained in the family ever since. The Verdea so often lauded by nineteenth-century travellers most probably came from their vineyards. At least when young, this wine has a pronounced greenish hue. June and her husband once made some at their home in Zakynthos and when they drew the first glass from the barrel, it was brilliant green and looked distinctly unappetizing. As it ages, however, it turns amber.

In the past, Zakynthos wines delivered a real punch, with an alcohol content of up to 15 percent. Judging by descriptions they seem to have resembled a tawny port or sherry. Winemakers today are changing these characteristics to meet modern tastes for drier, lighter wine. When you see references to Verdea in the recipes, we are talking about the old-style Verdea. Sherry would be a good substitute.

Miles Lambert-Gocs, who has written an authoritative guide to Greek wines, calls Verdea a "bouillabaisse of wine," because so many different types of grapes go into it. He cites a poem written in 1601 that mentions some thirty-four varieties grown on the island. Ludwig Salvator, some three hundred years later, tracked down eighty! While nowhere near that number exists today, Zakynthos does produce some reds and rosés, as well as the various mixtures of Verdea, but they hardly ever leave the island. When they do, they don't benefit from the trip. The Comoútos wines, should you find one, go well with game.

CEPHALONIA

Cephalonian wines are the best in the Ionian and among the best in Greece. Two names stand out here, the Calligá winery established in the early 1960s and Gentilíni, a newcomer on the market. Calligá produces a Robóla, a crisp, dry white wine that Lambert-Gocs compares favorably to a white bordeaux, plus a couple of reds. Gentilíni specializes in what Nico Manessis's *Greek Wine Guide* calls "new world wine, unlike anything Greece has ever produced." It, too, is white and clean-tasting. You might be able to find these wines at some dealers in the United States, though most of the vintage is exported to Britain.

Cephalonia is the only Ionian island that has been awarded the right to not one but three appellation of origin entitlements for its Robóla, Mavrodáphne, and Muscat wines. Comparable to the French *"appellation d'origine controlée,"* this means that the wines are from a specific region and grape, produced in a specified manner, and conform to certain standards governing sugar and alcohol content. Though its Muscat and Mavrodáphne output is negligible, there are many local wineries producing Robóla besides the two firms just mentioned. If you go to Cephalonia, you can find Robóla straight from the barrel in many a taverna or bottled by the winegrowers' cooperative. For some reason, Robóla bottles, whatever their provenance, are often dressed in some kind of sackcloth—burlap or blue.

LEFKADA

The vine the Venetians brought to Lefkada produces a thick, dark red wine similar to an Italian brusco. It is so dark the Lefkadians simply call it *chróma* or color, and it is so strong and dry that it almost clings to the roof of your mouth. Though a decent red wine on its own, it was in great demand in France and Italy for deepening the hues of their paler wines. It also gives color to their aperitifs, such as vermouth.

Though the Lefkadian wine tradition goes back to antiquity, the wines it produces today are little known outside the island. It has no single winery but a strong cooperative called TAOL, which stands for the Fund for the Defense of the Wine Producers of Lefkada. They joined together in 1928 to protect themselves from foreign exploitation.

CORFU

Lawrence Durrell and his drinking companions spent long hours discussing the merits of Corfiot wines. And there are hundreds of them, almost as many as there are country houses. As on the other islands, every village will have several individuals and tavernas with their own barrels. Some of them will even have made their wine the old-fashioned way, stamped on by bare feet in a vat and then poured into barrels to ferment. No matter what it tastes like, the proprietor is invariably proud of it.

The most prevalent grape is called *kakotrígos*. This literally means "hard to harvest." The stalk wraps itself around the vine and parts from the grape with difficulty, too. It produces a russet-colored wine, with a taste that Corfiots seem to appreciate but which outsiders have to acquire. Its alcohol content can also be quite high.

The most famous vineyard here is run by a member of the aristo-cratic Theotokis family in the Ropa Valley in the middle of the island. He produces both a white and an amber *kakotrígi* in fairly small amounts. Reds and so-called black wines are found in the north, other whites in the south. They rarely make an appearance in restaurants.

ITHACA AND PAXOS

Though you have to go there to sample them, the wines of these islands are excellent, but not commercially made.

GREEK DRINKING HABITS

The Greeks love to drink wine but they are very casual about it. They have no hard and fast rules about reds with meat and whites with fish. Nor are the various vineyards well enough established to have given birth to wine snobs. Few people talk about years and vintages. They just like something that tastes good and complements what they are eating. They have words like "*kráso mezé*" or "*bekrí mezé*," for dishes that seem to encourage the flow of wine and conviviality. Wine is simply a part of everyday life, drunk in moderation with every meal and perhaps enjoyed to excess on special occasions.

BASIC RECIPES
(Vasikés Syntaghés)

Tomato Sauce for Pasta
Sáltsa domáta yia makarónia

1 pound (¹/₂ kg.) fresh ripe tomatoes,
    peeled, halved, and grated
1 tablespoon olive oil
2 tablespoons butter
2 bay leaves
2 large basil leaves or 2 sprigs mint

2 garlic cloves, crushed (optional)
sugar to taste
salt to taste
freshly ground black pepper to taste
cayenne pepper to taste (optional)

Place all ingredients in a saucepan and simmer until sauce thickens —
about 30 minutes. Sufficient for 1 pound (¹/₂ kg.) pasta.

Simple Olive Oil and Lemon Sauce

Sáltsa ladolémono

This sauce is always served with grilled fish. It makes the fish succulent, tastier, and moister.

½ cup (120 ml.) olive oil   *½ teaspoon oregano (optional)*
¼ cup (60 ml.) lemon juice

Beat all ingredients well together and serve. *Serves 4.*

Pastry for Savory Pies

1 pound (½ kg.) all-purpose flour   *⅔ cup (160 ml.) warm olive oil*
1 teaspoon salt   *1 cup (240 ml.) warm wine*
1 teaspoon cinnamon (optional)

Sift flour, salt, and cinnamon together into a large bowl. Pour the olive oil on top. Then rub it into the flour mixture with your fingers. Make a well in the center of the flour. Pour the wine into it and mix with your hand. You should have a softish pliable dough—add more wine if necessary. This is sufficient for a round baking tin 12 inches (30 cm.) in diameter.

Short Crust Pastry

Suitable for Sweet and Savory Pies or Tarts

1 pound (½ kilo) all-purpose flour   *¾ pound (350 g.) butter (or half*
½ teaspoon salt   *butter and half margarine)*
                                              5 tablespoons water

Sift the flour and salt together into a bowl. Rub in the butter until the mixture becomes like fine breadcrumbs. Sprinkle the water over it and with a couple of knives mix together until a stiffish dough is formed. It may be necessary to add a little more water but be careful not to add too much. Wrap in foil or cellophane wrap and let it sit in the refrigerator for at least 30 minutes before rolling out.

Mayonnaise
Mayonéza

2 egg yolks

1/4 teaspoon salt

1–2 teaspoons mustard (preferably Dijon)

3/4 cup (180 ml.) sunflower oil

1/4 cup (60 ml) olive oil

lemon juice to taste

2 egg whites (optional)

Using either a food processor or an electric hand mixer, beat the egg yolks, salt, and mustard together and then slowly add the oils until the mixture thickens. At this point add the lemon juice and the rest of the oils alternately. Taste and adjust the seasonings. For a lighter variation add fresh herbs, either parsley, dill, or mint. You can also add chopped capers and gherkins.

Béchamel Sauce
Sáltsa besamél

3 tablespoons butter

3 tablespoons flour

3 cups (720 ml.) hot milk

nutmeg to taste

salt to taste

freshly ground black pepper to taste

Melt the butter in a saucepan and stir in the flour. Simmer for a minute or two and then, off the fire, add the hot milk all at once. With a wire whisk stir to remove any lumps until the sauce is smooth. Season with nutmeg, salt, and pepper. Cook for about 5 minutes more, stirring all the while.

Honey Syrup

1 1/2 cups (360 g.) honey

1/2 cup (100 g.) sugar

1 cinnamon stick

1/2 cup (120 ml.) water

Put all the ingredients in a saucepan and bring to the boil, stirring constantly. Simmer for about 5 minutes. Use for the *Tiganítes / Loukoumádes* on page 221, the *Díples* on page 222, and for cakes and sweet pies.

Egg-Lemon Sauce
Sáltsa avgolémono

This sauce is made with the liquid in which either *dolmádes* (stuffed vine or cabbage leaves), lamb fricassee (cooked with endive, artichokes or other greens), or *youvarlákia* (meatballs) are cooked in. Or it can be made with meat or chicken stock, or, in a pinch, with bouillon cubes diluted in water. It is a delicious sauce to serve over plain pilaff. The flour used in this recipe keeps the sauce from curdling.

1 tablespoon butter	*1 tablespoon lemon juice*
1 tablespoon flour	*1–2 eggs, beaten*
2 cups (480 ml.) stock	*salt to taste*
1 cup (240 ml.) milk	*freshly ground black pepper to taste*

Melt the butter in a saucepan and add the flour and cook for a few minutes. Then add the hot stock, stirring well, and then add the milk and stir again. Simmer for about 5 minutes and then stir in the lemon juice. Remove from the burner to cool a little and stir in the beaten eggs. Season with salt and pepper and simmer for a few more minutes, stirring all the time.

Infallible Egg-Lemon Soup

12 cups chicken, fish, or meat stock or soup	*juice of 2 lemons (or more, to taste)*
	salt to taste
2 eggs, separated	*freshly ground black pepper to taste*

Remove the soup from the heat. In a large bowl beat 2 egg whites until fairly stiff, then beat the yolks in a separate bowl. Add the lemon juice very slowly to the yolks, beating constantly. Now stir this mixture slowly into the egg whites. Add two cups of the broth to the egg-lemon bowl, again very slowly, still stirring. Pour this liquid, a bit at a time, back into the remaining soup, stirring in one direction. Season with salt and pepper and reheat without allowing the soup to boil. Do not cover the saucepan or the soup may curdle. (It will still taste fine, but it won't look very appetizing.)

THE BEST OF
ISLAND COOKING

How I wish the sea was wine
And the mountains were dainty morsels
And the boats were crystal glasses
For all the lovers of fun to use.

Very old Zakynthos song

APPETIZERS, SⁿUPS, AND SALADS
(Mezeδákia, Soúpes, kai Salátes)

APPETIZERS

Mezeδákia

Although for generations people in the Ionian Islands ate their meals Italian style, with a first course of pasta or soup, followed by a main course, they also have all the tidbits (*mezédes, mezedákia*) that Greeks like to sip wine or ouzo with. They also have several not found in the rest of the country. Some of these are the humble snacks of country people that savor of simple, hard-earned pleasures, others are sophisticated concoctions that would have been served at a formal dinner party.

Cod-Roe Dip

Taramosaláta

🏛 CORFU

No Greek cookbook would be complete without a recipe for this Lenten favorite that has become an hors d'oeuvre for all seasons.

Most people make it with bread soaked in water and then squeezed. But this recipe Diana happened upon in Gastoúri makes the fluffiest taramosaláta we have ever eaten.

4 slices day-old sandwich bread (not the Wonder variety) or any white peasant bread, crusts removed
3 ¹/₂ ounces (100 g.) cod-roe paste (taramopoltós)

¹/₄ cup (60 ml.) water
³/₄ cup (180 ml.) olive oil
1 small grated onion
lemon juice to taste

Crumble the bread in a blender or food processor. Remove. Have the olive oil and water ready and put the tarama paste in the processor container with a couple of tablespoons of the bread crumbs. Add the water, oil, and the rest of the bread crumbs, separately, little by little, until the mixture is pale and fluffy, not too fishy tasting and no more oil or water can be absorbed. Add the grated onion and lemon juice to season, whirr them for a few more seconds and if the taramosaláta is not fluffy enough add a bit more water. Serve as a dip with fresh country bread or raw vegetables. *Makes a medium-sized bowlful.*

Herring Roe Dip

Taramosaláta me avgá réngas

🏛 CORFU

This a Corfiot variant of the preceding recipe. It calls for smoked herring roe. These shiny golden fish can be found in Greek grocery stores. Ask the grocer to select two for you that have eggs. He can tell by prodding them with his fingers. In Zakynthos, one of the names for this fish is "the lawyer" (*dikigóros*) because it has the same shape as the redingote or tails that lawyers used to wear.

We use the conventional soaked bread here, but why not try it with dry crumbs, oil, and water as described above, if you prefer.

roe from 2 *smoked herrings*	*1 cup olive oil*
½ loaf day-old Greek or Italian bread	*juice of 1 lemon*

When you get the fish home, take the roe out of them and remove the membrane that surrounds it. Then mash the eggs thoroughly with a mortar and pestle, or—if you don't have one—with a wooden spoon (the food processor will not get them fine enough).

To make the dip, first soak 2 to 3 large chunks of crustless day-old peasant bread in water until they are saturated. Then squeeze them as dry as possible. Crumble the bread into the mortar with the roe or combine in a food processor, and then slowly add about a cupful of olive oil, as you would for a mayonnaise, until the mixture is smooth. Then add the juice of one lemon, more if desired, and serve with fresh bread.

With this version of *taramosaláta*, you've also got some fish to eat, which are very good topped with raw onion, sliced paper thin, and sprinkled with olive oil and lemon juice. Or you can serve them accompanied by hot, buttered boiled potatoes for an informal snack. The cold fish and the hot potato complement each other well.

Some people scorch the herring over a burner to remove the skin more easily, and others wrap it in newspaper and set it alight, but it can be removed without resorting to fire. The fish can also be used to make a non-Ionian mousse or pureed with horseradish and yogurt into another dip.

Pickled Octopus

Ktapódi toursí

🏛 CORFU

The slap-slap of an octopus being beaten against the rocks is heard frequently along Greek shores. To tenderize it, the fisherman must beat it at least a hundred times. Freezing tenderizes it, too, so if you buy a fresh one that hasn't been beaten, you can always stick it in the freezer for a day or two.

1 fresh or frozen octopus, about 2–3 lb. (1–1½ kg.)
vinegar

3 bay leaves
1 teaspoon hot red pepper
2 dried chili peppers, whole

Place the octopus in a nonstick saucepan and cook over low heat until tender. It should exude plenty of liquid, so don't add any water unless it starts to stick. Remove and cut into bite-sized pieces and place them in a glass jar. Measure enough vinegar to cover the octopus and pour it into a saucepan. Boil the vinegar together with the bay leaves, pepper, and chilis for about 10 minutes. Cool and pour over octopus. Close the jar and leave the octopus to marinate for about three days before eating. This is delicious with ouzo or wine. *Serves 6 to 8.*

Baked Octopus

Ktapódi psitó sto foúrno

🏛 KYTHERA

This easy recipe produces a succulent dish with a bare minimum of washing up.

1 medium sized octopus
½ cup (120 ml.) wine vinegar or wine (red or white)
2 tablespoons olive oil

2 bay leaves
3 cloves of garlic, unpeeled
freshly ground black pepper
oregano

Place the octopus in a bowl and pour the vinegar or wine over it. Leave to marinate at least half an hour, turning once or twice. Preheat the oven to 375° F. (190° C.) Tear off a long sheet of aluminum foil and lay the octopus on it along with the olive oil, bay leaves, garlic, and pepper. Wrap the foil around the octopus securely, place the packet in a roasting pan, and bake for about one hour. Cut the octopus into bite-sized pieces and serve with its juices, hot or cold, sprinkled with a little oregano.

Sea Urchin Salad

Achinosaláta

🏛 LEFKADA

This represents the height of luxury when you think that sea urchins cost about 5 francs ($1) apiece in Paris. But if you happen to be near a rocky shore in the Ionian, they can be plucked, gingerly, for nothing. The edible sea urchins are not black but various shades of dark green, reddish-brown, and mauve; their spines are often crowned by some small object, usually a shell or stone. Who knows how it gets there? Inside the intimidating carapace are five segments of eggs, whose color may range from bright yellow to brownish, and bits of what looks like seaweed. There are special cutters for slicing the shells in half, or use nail scissors or a paring knife.

eggs from 30–40 sea urchins
1 quart sea water

2–3 tablespoons olive oil
juice of 1 lemon

For this recipe you will need about 30 to 40 sea urchins for four people. Once you have exposed the eggs, discard the rest of the shell's contents, rinse with sea water if possible, and put the eggs in a bowl. When you have cleaned them all, pour over some olive oil and lemon juice, and let stand at least 10 minutes. The Lefkadians like to add a little chopped onion and garlic to this salad, but while delicious it does tend to mask the subtle flavor of the urchins.

Grilled Artichokes

Angináres psités sta kárvouna

🏛 KYTHERA

Wild artichokes grow in profusion all over the Greek countryside. Their leaves are topped with spikes but they have practically no "choke." In Kythera and Zakynthos these grilled artichokes used to be sold in the streets, to cries of *"angináres mámalo"* (as tender as can be). They are eaten leaf by leaf dipped in coarse salt.

cultivated or wild artichokes   *olive oil*
coarse sea salt

Choose medium-sized artichokes. Cut off the stalks, wash well, and drain. Sprinkle with salt and pour olive oil between the leaves. Grill over a charcoal fire, turning from time to time, until the leaves pull out easily.

Fried Artichokes

Angináres tiganités

🏛 CORFU

Anyone who has only eaten artichokes by the leaf cannot imagine the sybaritic pleasure of consuming as many as one likes during the extended Greek season. On the other hand, it is very hard to train oneself to peel and throw away all those uneaten outer leaves.

6 artichokes   *2 tablespoons flour*
lemon juice   *freshly ground black pepper to taste*
salt to taste   *½ cup (45 g.) grated kefalotýri (or*
2 eggs, beaten   *any sharp) cheese*

Allow 2 artichokes per person. Pare away all the tough outer leaves, cut in halves, remove choke, and cut each half into slices about ½–inch (1 cm.) thick. Parboil with the juice of a lemon and salt to taste added to the water. Drain.

Beat the flour, eggs, pepper, and cheese together to make a batter. Dip the artichoke slices into it and fry in hot oil in batches. Drain on paper towels and serve. *Serves 3.*

Eggplant Dip
Melitzanosaláta
🏛 CORFU

This recipe came from a Corfiot whose husband detests garlic and onions. A modern version of eggplant salad, it looks like avocado dip and has a very delicate flavor. A useful staple to keep in the fridge for unexpected guests or as a sandwich spread.

2 *medium round eggplants*
juice of 2 lemons
1/2 *cup (120 ml.) olive oil*
1/4 *cup (60 ml.) vinegar*
2 *teaspoon Dijon mustard*

2 *tablespoons parsley, finely chopped*
salt to taste
freshly ground black pepper to taste
1 *egg yolk*

Prick the eggplants several times with a fork and grill for about 20 minutes over a gas burner, charcoal, or electric grill until the skins are charred and the eggplants are soft. This gives their flesh a delectable smoky taste. Hold the eggplant by the stem and remove all the charred skin. It is easier to remove the skin when the eggplant is hot and if you peel it from the bottom up towards the stem. Rinse the flesh quickly under the cold water tap.

Place cleaned eggplant in a colander and immediately squeeze the juice of 2 lemons over it. Set aside for an hour to allow the excess liquid to drain away. Then squeeze the eggplant with your hands or with a piece of cheesecloth to remove any additional liquid. Next, combine all the ingredients except the egg yolk in a blender or food processor at medium speed for about 1 minute, add egg yolk and blend another few seconds. Taste and adjust the seasoning. Serve with thin slices of brown bread or crackers. *Serves 6 to 8.*

Eggplant Salad

Melitzanosaláta

🏛 CORFU

Another version of the Greek classic, this one has hard-boiled eggs and finely chopped almonds to bind and flavor it.

2 pounds (1 kg.) large round eggplants
3 hard-boiled eggs, finely chopped
juice of 1 lemon
½ cup (120 ml.) olive oil
1 tablespoon vinegar

⅔ cup (85 g.) almonds, blanched and finely chopped
3 tablespoons parsley, finely chopped
salt to taste
freshly ground black pepper to taste

Cook the eggplant over direct heat—either gas, charcoal, or electric grill—until soft. Remove the charred skin of the eggplant (see preceding recipe), place the flesh together with all the other ingredients in a bowl, and mash with a fork until thoroughly blended. Serve with fresh bread and chilled white wine. *Serves 8 to 10.*

Sundried Tomatoes

Domátes iliópiastes

🏛 CORFU

The Corfiots dry their own tomatoes by the kilo. They just spread them outdoors on a flat surface, cut in half with some coarse salt sprinkled over them. Five days in the scorching summer sun is usually enough to shrink them to stiff, chewy morsels. They then place them in jars, pour olive oil over them, and save them for livening up sauces and soups in the winter.

They also fry them to make a delicious and unusual dip.

First soak some dried tomatoes in water to get rid of any excess salt and to allow them to reabsorb some liquid. Drain and dry them. Toss in flour and fry in hot oil until they puff up into little red bubbles. Drain on paper towels and devour.

A FAVORITE CORFIOT SNACK

A fat slice of fresh country bread smeared with olive oil and the juice of half a tomato, sprinkled with *rígani* (oregano) and salt is what mothers give their hungry children in Corfu. When the children have left the kitchen, they often make one for themselves as well.

TWO FAVORITE ITHACAN SNACKS

In summer the Ithacans love to nibble on stale whole wheat bread that they slice and sprinkle with a little water to soften. They then crumble it and make a "salad" of it, tossing it in oil and vinegar, chopped garlic, and *rígani*. This they call either *riganáda* or *ncrobábuli*. In winter, they make *tzoúpa*, bread toasted on the fire and soaked in a mixture of olive oil and wine. They maintain that it marries perfectly with cheese and keeps melancholy at bay. (These snacks are also found in Zakynthos and Cephalonia.)

Fried Baby Potatoes

Patatoúles tiganités

🏛 CORFU

A lovely way to eat the smallest of new potatoes.

½ pound small new potatoes   *4 sprigs rosemary*
2 tablespoons olive oil

Wash, but do not peel potatoes. In a little olive oil fry the potatoes gently. Toss a few sprigs of rosemary in the frying pan just before they are ready.

Garlic Sauce/Dip

Skordaliá or Ayáda

🏛 KYTHERA

There are probably as many ways of making this wonderful sauce as there are Ionian islands, and of course the amount of garlic will depend on individual taste. The housewives of Cephalonia are reputed to make the best and strongest *skordaliá* in the Ionian. The local garlic bulbs are small, with pale purple skins, and extremely pungent; whereas those grown in Zakynthos are apt to be large, white, and much milder (like the California variety). Ideally, *skordaliá* should be made with a stone mortar and pestle, and should be so stiff that the pestle is able to lift up the mortar. However, a food processor is a very good substitute.

This sauce is traditionally served with fried salt cod on the 25th of March, Palm Sunday, and August 6th, but it is also eaten on many other occasions. It is good with any fish and also with boiled beets, greens, or fried eggplant and zucchini. Try it with other vegetables, too.

1 pound (¹/₂ kg.) potatoes, peeled	*1 cup (240 ml.) best quality olive oil*
3 or more cloves of garlic	*salt to taste*
¹/₂ cup (65 g.) almonds or walnuts	*¹/₃ cup (80 ml.) vinegar*

Boil the potatoes in salted water and drain, saving a little of the water. Place the garlic, nuts, half the oil, and some salt in a blender or food processor. Blend or process well and—with the blades turning—add the hot potatoes one by one, until you have a smooth puree. Then add the rest of the olive oil and the vinegar slowly, alternating the one and the other until both cups are empty. Add more salt if necessary.

The Corfiots, being garlic lovers in the extreme, make this dish with 2 to 3 heads of garlic, lemon juice instead of vinegar, and use a little water from the boiled potatoes to lighten the puree.

This recipe is from Kythera. To make a Cephalonian *skordaliá*, omit the nuts and increase the amount of garlic to one head or more. June herself never puts olive oil into the sauce, but serves it poured over the prepared *skordaliá* as her Zantiot mother-in-law taught her.

Tip: If you want your garlic to be less offensive to others, remove the green tip and core when making dishes where it is served raw (as in *skordaliá* for example). Even so, if might be more advisable to eat it over the weekend than on a working day.

Cheese and Garlic Dip

Féta kai skórdo mezé

🏛 CEPHALONIA

Feta, made with ewe's or cow's milk or a mixture of the two, is the quintessential Greek cheese. It has spread all over the world. June even found it in a remote Ethiopian village made by a local girl married to a Greek expatriate. (He'd have to have a been a Cephalonian; determined individualists, they're renowned for ending up in the most farflung places.)

Feta and garlic go surprisingly well together, and this is a quick meze to serve with a *vin ordinaire*. In Cephalonia, you'd be drinking some *Robóla* from the barrel.

½ pound (225 g.) feta	*2 tablespoons olive oil*
2 cloves garlic, mashed	*⅓ teaspoon oregano*

Place feta in a bowl and mash well. Add the rest of the ingredients and mix together thoroughly or alternatively place all ingredients in a food processor and whirr on slow speed until smooth. Serve with crackers or slices of fresh country bread. *Serves 6 to 8.*

Fried Fresh Garlic

Skórda tsigaristá

🏛 ITHACA

If you are lucky enough to find fresh garlic or grow it in your garden, this recipe is too easy and delicious not to try.

5 fresh garlic stems	1 tablespoon tomato paste
2 tablespoons olive oil	salt to taste
1 cup white wine	freshly ground black pepper to taste

Cut the garlic stems into pieces about 2– to 3–inches long. Fry in olive oil gently until they soften. Mix white wine with the tomato paste, salt, and pepper. Add to the garlic stems, cover, and simmer until the liquid is absorbed. It is just possible that the Ithacans like garlic even more than the rest of the islanders do.

Marinated Mushrooms

Manitária marináta

🏛 ZAKYNTHOS

All of the islands have a variety of edible wild mushrooms, although cultivated ones will do almost as well for this dish. In his exhaustive study of Zakynthos in 1904, Ludwig Salvator reported that the islanders loved mushrooms: they ate them fried in olive oil, baked in the oven and served with a sauce of garlic and vinegar, or stewed with onions and wine. This is a modern recipe.

2 medium onions, finely chopped	1 teaspoon rosemary
4 tablespoons olive oil	salt to taste
1 pound (½ kg.) fresh ripe tomatoes,	freshly ground black pepper to taste
skinned, seeded, halved and grated	2 pounds (1 kg.) fresh mushrooms
2 cloves garlic, finely chopped	2 tablespoons lemon juice

Sauté the onion in 2 tablespoons of the olive oil until soft and golden and then add the tomatoes, garlic, rosemary, salt, and pepper. Simmer until the liquid evaporates and you have a thick sauce. Clean mushrooms with as little water as possible, dry, and cut in two. Pour the lemon juice over them and leave for 10 minutes. Sauté them in the remaining olive oil. Add to the sauce and simmer for 10 more minutes. May be eaten hot or cold. *Serves 6 to 8.*

Yellow Split Pea Puree Dip
Fáva
🏛 ALL ISLANDS

This is a great favorite all over Greece, in both homes and tavernas. Many years ago and up to the 1930s *fáva* was sold from cauldrons in the streets of Zakynthos. Vendors used to shout *"zestós eínai o fávas"* (the *fáva* is hot). For some reason in Zakynthos it is a masculine noun while in the rest of Greece its gender is feminine. *Fáva* can also be eaten hot as a thick soup.

The Kytherans have a dish called *pandreméni fáva*, leftover puree "married" to—fried with—tomato paste.

2 cups (400 g.) yellow split peas	**GARNISHES**
1 large onion, cut in chunks	*olive oil*
2 tablespoons olive oil	*lemon wedges*
salt to taste	*cayenne pepper (optional)*
freshly ground black pepper to taste	*chopped onion*
	olives (optional)

Place the split peas in a saucepan together with the onion and olive oil and cover with cold water. Boil the peas until they are tender and the water has almost evaporated. Mash peas well and if you want a very smooth consistency puree them in a food processor. Season with salt and pepper. When this cools it becomes quite solid. Spread the puree on a serving dish and sprinkle with olive oil. Serve accompanied by lemon wedges, cayenne pepper, chopped onion, olives, and more olive oil. *Serves 6 to 8.*

Fried Zucchini Flowers

Kolokithokorfádeſ

🏛 ALL ISLANDS

The bright yellow-orange flowers of the zucchini are much too pretty to discard, and they make a delicious hors d'oeuvre. Though they are sometimes served stuffed with rice on the mainland, the Ionian Greeks often dip them in batter and fry them, as do the Italians.

If the batter is made with beer instead of water, and each flower has a caper placed in its heart, the result is even tastier. Wash the flowers and remove the stamens, pistils, and fringe at the bottom before dipping them in a light, seasoned batter. Fry in sizzling oil.

SOUPS

Soúpes

The majority of the soups included here show the Ionians' passion for pulses (*óspria*). Served at least twice a week in most households, they are thick, robust soups. If you are aghast at the amount of olive oil used to cook them, you'll be even more horrified to learn that it is customary to pour even more oil over the individual servings. Reduce the quantities if you like, but the oil really does make them tastier.

Tomato Soup for Lent

Domatósoupa yia Sarakostí

🏛 ZAKYNTHOS

Sarakostí comes from *saránda*, the Greek word for forty, identifying that this dish is appropriate for Lent. There is no hint of deprivation in this tomato soup; it even includes a liberal dose of wine.

2 pounds (1 kg.) tomatoes, skinned, seeded, and grated

3 cups (720 ml.) water

2–3 cloves garlic, flattened but whole

1 teaspoon sugar

1 cup (240 ml.) red or white wine

2 tablespoons celery, finely chopped

1/2 cup (120 ml.) olive oil

1 medium onion

salt to taste

freshly ground black pepper to taste

6 tablespoons orzo or another small pasta

Place tomatoes and water in a saucepan and bring to the boil. Add all the other ingredients except the pasta and simmer for about 20 minutes. Discard the onion and garlic, add the pasta, and simmer until done. Add more water if soup becomes too thick. Adjust seasonings if necessary. *Serves 6.*

Fish Soup

Psarósoupa

🏛 ALL ISLANDS

This is an archetypal recipe of the sort perfected by the ancient Greeks (of course, the pepper, tomato, and potato would have been absent). Some purists maintain that potatoes cloud the broth. If you are one of them, boil the potatoes separately.

3–4 onions	*3 tablespoons lemon juice*
3–4 carrots	*9 cups (2 liters) water*
3 celery stalks	*2–3 pounds (1-1½ kg.) white fish, i.e.,*
2–3 bay leaves	*scorpion fish, dentex, sea bream,*
1 green pepper (optional)	*grouper, or grey mullet, or a mixture*
1 large ripe tomato (optional)	*6 or more medium potatoes, halved*
salt to taste	*6 tablespoons short grain rice*
freshly ground black pepper to taste	*2 tablespoons parsley, finely chopped*
3 tablespoons olive oil	*lemon wedges*

Place the onions, carrots, celery, bay leaves, green pepper and tomato (if used), salt, pepper, olive oil, and lemon juice in a large saucepan. Cover with water and boil vigorously for about 20 minutes. Add the cleaned fish with heads intact and potatoes, and boil until fish and potatoes are done. Strain. Return liquid to saucepan, bring to a boil, add the rice, and cook until the rice is soft. Reseason. Serve the soup sprinkled with parsley and accompanied by lemon wedges. Serve the fish and vegetables separately as the second course with mayonnaise or an oil-and-lemon sauce (see page 82). *Serves 6.*

Alternatively make an egg-lemon soup from the stock (see page 84).

Turkey Egg-Lemon Soup

Soúpa avgolémono apó galopoúla

🏛 ZAKYNTHOS

In the months preceding Christmas Zakynthos seems to be overrun with turkeys. The baby turkeys are brought over from the mainland and raised on a diet of windfall olives and other choice tidbits so that their flesh is juicy and tasty.

Turkey *avgolémono* soup is a traditional prelude to the Christmas lunch in both Corfu and Zakynthos. It is made from the wings, neck, and giblets. The following method of making egg-lemon sauce produces an extremely rich and creamy soup.

In another version of the recipe, the whole bird is boiled and then browned in the oven. The rich broth makes a delectable soup.

The Zakynthians always sprinkle grated cheese on their egg-lemon soup — a practice not found elsewhere in Greece.

12 cups (3 liters) of turkey broth, made from turkey parts — wings and giblets — or even from the entire carcass of a holiday turkey	*juice of 2 lemons*
	salt to taste
	freshly ground black pepper to taste
	½ cup kefalotýri, myzíthra, *or*
6 tablespoons short grain rice	Romano *cheese, grated (optional)*
2 eggs, separated	

Bring broth to the boil, add the rice, and cook until soft. Remove the saucepan from the heat. In a large bowl beat the egg whites until fairly stiff, then beat the yolks in a separate bowl. Very slowly add the lemon juice to the yolks, beating constantly. Stir this mixture slowly into the egg whites. Add two cups of the broth to the egg-lemon bowl, again very slowly, still stirring. Pour this liquid, a bit at a time, back into the remaining soup, stirring in one direction. Season with salt and pepper and reheat without allowing the soup to boil. Serve with grated cheese if desired. *Serves 6.*

Tip: Do not cover the saucepan or the soup may curdle. (It will still taste fine, but it won't look very appetizing.)

Chick-Pea Soup

Revithósoupa

🏛 CORFU

In classical times they used to sprinkle pomegranate seeds on this soup.

1 pound (¹/₂ kg.) chick-peas
several whole cloves — even a whole
*   head — garlic*
salt to taste
freshly ground black pepper to taste

1 teaspoon rosemary sprigs
¹/₃ cup (80 ml.) olive oil
1 medium potato, grated (optional)
1 or 2 lemons, juiced
1 teaspoon flour

Place the presoaked and washed chick-peas in a big kettle with at least twice as much water as chick-peas, together with several whole garlic cloves, salt, black pepper, rosemary, and olive oil. A little grated potato can be added to thicken the soup, if desired. Bring to a boil and simmer until tender. Discard any loose skins.

When the chick-peas are tender, add the lemon juice mixed with the flour to thicken and bring out the flavor. *Serves 6 to 8.*

Tip: Soak pulses, except for lentils and split yellow peas (*fáva*), overnight with a pinch of bicarbonate of soda. Discard water and rinse. Then, to avoid the flatulence that often makes pulses the "musical fruit," bring them to the boil with plenty of water, skim off foam, and then discard water. Rinse and bring them to the boil again with fresh water.

Zakynthos Bean Soup

Fasoláda

🏛 ZAKYNTHOS

In the old days street vendors in Zakynthos used to sell steaming bean soup from large cauldrons, as well as blocks of stiff yellow split pea puree. They would shout, "*Miá dekára sto boúrboula kai duó sti apoládia,*" which means: "A penny for the boiling bottom part of the soup and two for the top where the oil floats." June heard this story from an acquaintance whose grandfather went to Zakynthos in 1876 for his honeymoon.

Bean soup is a winter favorite throughout Greece. This Zakynthian version came from the mountains, where it is made either "red" or "white," i.e., with or without tomato.

1 pound (1/2 kg.) haricot beans
2–3 carrots, cubed
2–3 sticks celery, sliced
1 large or 2 medium onions, chopped
3 tablespoons dill or fennel, coarsely chopped
2 tablespoons parsley, coarsely chopped

1 cup (240 ml.) olive oil
1 tablespoon tomato paste (optional)
2 or 3 medium potatoes, grated
lemon juice to taste (optional)
salt to taste
freshly ground black pepper to taste

Place beans in a large saucepan and cover with cold water. Bring to a boil and then strain. Place beans in a clean saucepan and add the carrots, celery, onion, herbs, and fresh water to cover. Bring to a boil and simmer until beans are just tender. Add the olive oil and, if desired, tomato paste diluted in a little of the soup, and boil vigorously for about five minutes. Add the grated potato and continue to boil until the potato is soft. If you don't use tomato paste, stir in lemon juice to taste. Season with salt and pepper. *Serves 6.*

Tip: The beans do not need overnight soaking if they are less than a year old. Of course, some beans never get tender no matter how long you cook them. This may be because the water in your area is hard. If so, use bottled water or rain water for this purpose.

Lentil Soup

Soúpa fakí

🏛 LEFKADA

Lefkada was once the lentil capital of Greece. The dry, rocky earth around Englouví in the heart of the island produced the finest tasting pulses.

1 pound (¹/₂ kg.) brown lentils
2–3 bay leaves
3 cloves garlic, more if desired
1 cup (240 ml.) olive oil
1 tablespoon tomato paste

¹/₄ cup (60 ml.) vinegar, or less
1–2 teaspoon oregano
salt to taste
freshly ground black pepper to taste

Place the lentils, bay leaves, and garlic in a saucepan and cover with cold water. Bring to a boil and simmer until the lentils are nearly done. Add the olive oil and tomato paste mixed with some liquid from the lentils. Boil rapidly until the soup has thickened, then stir in the vinegar, oregano, salt, and pepper. *Serves 6.*

Multi-Bean Soup

Polyspória or Boubourélla

🏛 ITHACA

November 21st commemorates the Presentation or dedication of the Virgin by her parents to Solomon's temple, where she remained for twelve years before her betrothal to Joseph. In farming communities the celebration falls halfway through the sowing period. Combining the two ideas, there is a legend that after the ceremony Mary's mother distributed pulses and grains among the crowds waiting outside. Maria Kostára, a woman from Ithaca who celebrates her name day on the 21st, takes great pleasure in serving all her guests a bowl of them along with her other *mezédes*. They can be eaten either as soup or drained as a salad sprinkled with oil and either vinegar or lemon.

For this recipe you will need every kind of pulse you can lay your hands on.

½ cup (100 g.) whole wheat, husks
    removed
½ cup (100 g.) each chick-peas, lentils,
    green and yellow split peas, white
    beans, black-eyed peas, red beans, etc.
1 large onion, chopped

salt to taste
freshly ground black pepper to taste
½ cup (100 g.) frozen corn (this would
    not have been served at the temple)
olive oil
vinegar or lemon

Soak the wheat and the pulses that need it (all but the lentils and yellow peas) in water overnight. Drain.

The next day bring the chick-peas and wheat to the boil together in plenty of water and cook for about 30 minutes. Add the other ingredients, except the corn. When all of the vegetables are tender, throw in the corn and cook another 5 minutes. Serve as soup or drained as bean salad. Season both soup and salad with olive oil and vinegar or oil and lemon. *Serves 10 to 12.*

SALADS

(Saláteſ)

For the Greeks a salad is any vegetable raw, cooked, or combination thereof, tossed with olive oil and lemon or vinegar. Cauliflower, beets, pole beans (*ambelofásola*), greens of every kind, broccoli, and zucchini are all delicious boiled or steamed and given this simple treatment.

We have omitted the ubiquitous "Greek Peasant Salad" and have selected just a few raw salads that are not typical of the rest of Greece. For example, the peppery weed, arugula or "garden rocket," found in vacant lots all over Athens, is very rarely eaten on the Greek mainland. But the open-air market in Corfu is full of it, and it is a much-esteemed ingredient in salads there.

Romaine Lettuce and Walnut Salad

Saláta maroúli me karýdia

🏛 CORFU

Walnuts make a crunchy addition to this simple salad.

4 cups romaine, finely sliced
4 tablespoons dill, finely chopped
½ cup (150 g.) walnuts, coarsely chopped

1 tablespoon vinegar
3 tablespoons olive oil
salt to taste
pepper to taste

Mix all ingredients together and serve. *Serves 6.*

Cabbage and Arugula Salad

Krabí kai róka saláta

🏛 CORFU

1 cup white cabbage, shredded
1 cup carrots, grated
2 cups arugula, chopped
½ cup (150 g.) walnuts, coarsely chopped

1 tablespoon vinegar
1 tablespoon lemon juice
6 tablespoons olive oil
salt to taste

Mix all ingredients together and serve. *Serves 6.*

Fennel and Orange Salad

Saláta me finókio kai portokália

🏛 CORFU

This unusual salad is a creation of the Jews of Corfu. It is taken from Nicholas Stavroulakis's wonderful *Cookbook of the Jews of Greece*. Jews first emigrated to Corfu in the twelfth century. By 1386 they were such a significant part of the population that "David, son of Simon" was included in the six-man delegation that sailed to Venice to negotiate the terms of the island's takeover. Apart from working as bankers and tailors, many men worked as porters in Corfu's marketplace, while others ran the very profitable firm that rented the furnishings and livery to the Venetian governor in the eighteenth century. After their expulsion from Spain and Portugal during the Inquisition, Jewish refugees founded communities in Zakynthos and Lefkada, as well.

1 head romaine lettuce	*2 lemons, juiced*
1 large fennel bulb	*1 tablespoon honey or sugar*
1 large orange, peeled and thinly sliced	*salt to taste*
½ cup (120 ml.) olive oil	*freshly ground black pepper to taste*

Hold the lettuce in one hand and with the other cut it horizontally into thin shreds with a sharp knife. Put in a salad bowl. Cut the fennel into thin slices, including some of the feathery leaves, and lay these over the lettuce. Arrange the orange slices on top.

Put the olive oil, lemon juice, honey or sugar, salt, and pepper in a jar with a tight-fitting lid and shake vigorously until well mixed. Pour over the salad and toss well before serving. *Serves 4 to 6.*

Lentil and Potato Salad

Fakés kai patatosaláta

🏛 CEPHALONIA

This is a modern recipe for a useful salad to serve at an informal summer lunch party.

3/4 cup (150 g.) brown lentils
2 medium potatoes
3 slices ham, finely chopped
1/2 hot pickled chili pepper, finely chopped
2 tablespoons parsley, finely chopped
1 hard-boiled egg, coarsely chopped

4 gherkins, finely chopped
2 tablespoons olive oil
1 tablespoon vinegar
1 teaspoon prepared mustard
salt to taste
freshly ground black pepper to taste

Boil the lentils until just tender and drain. Boil the potatoes in their skins until just tender, peel, and cut into cubes. Mix all the ingredients together, taste, and adjust seasonings if necessary. *Serves 6*

Koula's Green Pepper and Potato Salad

Patatosaláta me piperiés

🏛 CORFU

Koula Kapsokavadi of Gastouri has a way of making even the most humble combinations memorable.

1 pound (1/2 kg.) new potatoes
2 plump green peppers
1/2 cup (120ml.) olive oil
3 tablespoons vinegar

salt to taste
freshly ground black pepper to taste
1/2 bunch parsley, chopped

Boil the potatoes in their skins until tender and drain. Cut the peppers in thin strips and parboil for about 5 minutes. Drain. Slice the potatoes and toss with the peppers in an oil and vinegar dressing. Sprinkle with chopped parsley and serve at room temperature. *Serves 4.*

CHEESE, EGGS, AND PASTA
(Tyrí, Avgá, kai Makarónia)

Though the Ionians add cheese to many of their dishes, they have very few recipes in which cheese is the featured ingredient.

The egg dishes represent beautiful marriages with garlic and tomatoes, while the pasta recipes are surprisingly typical of almost anywhere else in Greece. In spite of having been under the Venetian wing for so many centuries, the Ionians have remarkably few pasta dishes and sauces to go with them. They stick to the old standbys — spaghetti with meat or tomato sauce and angel hair pasta in soups for invalids. They are also especially partial to thick macaroni (not elbow but full length), which appears as an accompaniment to many of their favorite dishes.

Cheese Pie Without Trousers

Tyrópita avrákoti

🏛 CEPHALONIA

The name is a local witticism referring to the pie's lack of crust. Called a pie, this is really a cheese bread that contains very little flour. It resembles a flat soufflé but is very light and tasty. This is a very versatile recipe; try experimenting with different kinds of cheese.

4 tablespoons softened butter
3 eggs
2 cups (200 g.) feta cheese, grated
2 tablespoon kefalotýri, *Romano, or Parmesan cheese, grated*

½ cup (120 ml.) strained yogurt (see page 66)
½ cup (75 g.) sifted flour
1 teaspoon baking powder

Preheat the oven to 450° F. (230° C.). Beat the butter until pale and fluffy and add the eggs one at a time, beating well. Add the rest of the ingredients and beat well again. Pour the batter into a buttered 10-inch (25-cm.) baking tin and bake for 10 minutes. Then lower heat to 400° F. (205° C.) and continue baking for half an hour. *Serves 6.*

Scrambled Eggs with Tomatoes

Avgá strapadsáda

🏛 ZAKYNTHOS

This a quick and easy solution for a casual lunch or supper. Kids love it served with french fries.

1½ pounds (¾ kg.) ripe tomatoes, skinned, halved, and grated
4 tablespoons olive oil
salt to taste

pepper to taste
½ teaspoon sugar
8 eggs

Place the grated tomatoes and the olive oil in a large frying pan and season with salt, pepper, and sugar. Simmer until the tomato juice evaporates and the oil separates from the tomatoes. Break the eggs into the sauce, stirring to mix well, and cook gently over a low heat until firm. Adjust seasonings if necessary and serve at once. *Serves 6 to 8.*

Eggs Smothered in Garlic

Avgá skordostoúmbi

🏛 ZAKYNTHOS

This is a convenient summer dish that requires no planning since all the ingredients are likely to be on hand. It's also a great favorite with children. Add more garlic if it appeals to you.

¹/₄ cup (60 ml.) olive oil
6 eggs
4 cloves garlic, thinly sliced
1 tablespoon tomato paste diluted in 1 cup (240 ml.) water [or 1 pound (¹/₂ kg.) ripe tomatoes, halved and grated]

salt and pepper to taste
sugar to taste (optional)
1 pound (¹/₂ kg.) potatoes, peeled and sliced as for french fries

Sauté the garlic lightly in olive oil, then add the diluted tomato paste or the tomatoes and season with salt, pepper, and sugar (if desired). Bring the sauce to a boil and then add the potatoes. Simmer until the potatoes are done, adding hot water if they begin to stick. With a slotted spoon remove potatoes to a hot plate, then break the eggs into the sauce, and simmer until set. *Serves 3 or more, depending on your appetite.*

Piquant Poached Eggs

Avgá me domáta sáltsa

🏛 CEPHALONIA

Here's another version of eggs and tomatoes that also calls for a great deal of garlic, but requires the addition of cheese and wine as well, which make the dish richer and more piquant. It seems to cry out for large quantities of fresh bread and wine, and it is even better eaten beside a view of the sea surrounded by the aroma of pine trees.

Perhaps it was a dish like this that caused English aristocrats to travel into the Ionian countryside with their own cooks, who would make plain English meals with ingredients provided by their hosts. As Kirkwall wrote in 1863, "Thus you escape the oil and garlic flavor which usually permeates all native cookery. The garlic grown in the island is insufficient for home consumption and I was assured that, to supply the deficiency, 25,000 l. [*sic*] worth of the unsavory comestible is annually imported into Cephalonia."

Without the eggs this also makes an excellent sauce for spaghetti.

3 tablespoons olive oil

2 pounds (1 kg.) ripe tomatoes, halved and grated

2 heads garlic, finely chopped (less if desired)

1/2 cup (120 ml.) white or red wine

1/2 teaspoon sugar

3 tablespoons (50 g.) feta, crumbled

2–3 tablespoons (50 g.) kefalotýri, Romano, or Parmesan cheese, grated

salt to taste

pepper to taste

8 eggs

Heat the oil in a frying pan, add the tomatoes and garlic, and cook over a high heat to bring out and reduce the tomato juices. Then, lowering the heat, add the wine, sugar, and cheeses. Simmer to reduce to a fairly thick sauce and season sparingly with salt and pepper. Break the eggs into the sauce, cover pan, and simmer until the eggs are set. *Serves 4 or more.*

Macaroni with False Ragout Sauce

Makarónia me pséftiki sáltsa

🏛 ZAKYNTHOS

This Lenten dish was a great favorite of June's brother-in-law. He always prepared it on the Monday before Easter. Of course, cheese was not allowed, but rusk crumbs made a good substitute.

Under the name *pseftósoupa* or "false soup" something akin to this dish is eaten in Lefkada and Corfu. On Good Friday even the oil is omitted.

3 medium onions, sliced

3 tablespoons olive oil

2 pounds (1 kg.) ripe tomatoes, halved and grated (or a large can of tomatoes, peeled and chopped)

2 bay leaves

3 cloves

3 cinnamon sticks

salt to taste

freshly ground pepper to taste

1 pound macaroni or other thick pasta rusk crumbs

Sauté the onions in the olive oil and then add the rest of the ingredients, except the macaroni and rusk crumbs. Simmer until you have a thickish sauce. Boil the macaroni until al dente and serve it with the sauce and rusk crumbs instead of grated cheese. *Serves 4.*

FISH
(Psári)

Strange that on most of these islands fish should be such a luxury. Nevertheless, many of the visitors over the past two centuries have commented on the expense of fresh fish and described the excitement when a caïqueful would arrive from the lagoon fisheries of Missolonghi or Preveza on the mainland.

Instead, one finds many recipes for salt cod, that staple of the days before refrigeration. Shellfish and shrimp are also rare; while tourists feast on lobster at Paleokastrítsa in Corfu, it does not seem to appear in Ionian traditional cooking. The octopus and its relatives, squid and cuttlefish, are plentiful.

One reason there are comparatively few fish recipes is that the best ways to deal with a fresh fish are simple (and the same the world over): just boil it in a flavored broth, or fry, steam, or grill it with a little olive oil, lemon juice, and a sprinkling of herbs.

The Ithacans say that a bride should never eat fish on her wedding day or else she'll flip and flop from man to man as frantically as a fish out of water.

Marinated Fish

Savoúro or *Savóro*

🏛 ALL ISLANDS

This recipe has an Italian sounding name and lives on in the Venetian dish *sardelle in saor*, which may hark back to Byzantium, since it is known in so many other regions of Greece. It may even date from ancient times; the Romans, after all, started the sweet and sour trend by combining currants and vinegar. In any case, it was perfected well before the advent of the refrigerator, when fish were plentiful and cheaper. Before the Second World War families used to cook more fish than they could eat at one sitting, so they could feast on this delicacy for the rest of the week. Shops in the towns once made it by the barrel, and the women of Ithaca used to ship it off to their husbands and sons, who worked on the Danube riverboats.

The ideal fish for this recipe is red mullet (*barboúnia*) but cheaper fish will also do nicely. In the Ionian large picarel (*marídes*), or *góppes*, which have the unlikely scientific name of *Boops boops*, are often used. In the U.S. you could use any smallish fish that you fry, even fresh sardines as the Venetians do.

This dish is traditionally eaten during Lent, especially on March 25th (the Annunciation of the Virgin) and Palm Sunday.

2 pounds (1 kg.) small fish	1/2 cup (50 g.) currants (optional)
4–5 heaping tablespoons flour	6 cloves garlic, finely chopped
salt to taste	2 tablespoons rosemary
pepper to taste	1 tablespoon black peppercorns
1/2 cup olive oil, plus 2 tablespoons	1 cup (240 ml.) vinegar

Clean and gut fish. Dredge them in flour seasoned with salt and pepper and fry fish in olive oil. Drain on absorbent paper and set aside. If you have the time, let them cool, even overnight, because they will then absorb the marinade more quickly.

In a clean frying pan, heat 2 tablespoons of olive oil and sauté the currants, garlic, rosemary, and peppercorns for 1 minute until the currants puff up. Then pour in the vinegar. When it comes to the boil, add the fried fish and cook for one minute. Remove from fire.

Pour into a pyrex dish with a cover, making sure the marinade covers the fish. Keep in a cool place. This should stand at least 48 hours to marinate fully. It will keep for at least a month—it gets better and better as the month wears on and the vinegar permeates the fish, but you might not be able to hold off eating it sooner. Serve with slices of fresh brown bread and butter. *Serves 6 to 8.*

FISH STEWS
(Bourdéttos)

Bourdétto is an obvious corruption of the Venetian word *"brodetto,"* meaning soup or broth. The dish, which is more a stew than a soup, is unique to Corfu and Paxos, where there are several versions of it, all featuring plenty of hot red pepper. Curiously, none of the other Ionian islands use red pepper or chilis in their cooking. Nor is it used much in Greek mainland cooking, except in the north. As the closest island to the area, Corfu may have received more refugees from Macedonia and Thrace when the Turks took over those provinces. Or it may have arrived via Dubrovnik, another Venetian-controlled town just up the Adriatic, which had contact with paprika-loving areas in the Balkans. All Corfiot grocers sell ready-made packets of cayenne and paprika used in these popular dishes.

This recipe calls for either salt cod or wind-dried cod. The latter is known as stockfish (*stoccafisso* in Italian, *stakofisi* in Corfiot), and colloquially as stickfish (*bastounópsaro*), because it is so hard. When thoroughly rinsed of salt it has a pleasant taste and firm texture.

Salt Cod Stew

Bakaliáro bourdétto

🏛 CORFU

For this recipe and the one that follows; you can substitute fresh or frozen cod fillets. Or cook as the Corfiots do; omit the fish altogether, leaving you with two delicious vegetable dishes.

3 pounds (1¹/₂ kg.) salt cod
1 cup (240 ml.) olive oil
2 tablespoons cayenne pepper
1 medium onion, chopped
1 head garlic, finely chopped
1 tomato, peeled, seeded and chopped
    (or 1 teaspoon tomato paste—
    more for color than taste)

2 pounds (1 kg.) potatoes, peeled and
    quartered
1 cup (60 ml.) water
¹/₂ tablespoon black pepper
chopped parsley for garnish

Shake the loose salt off the codfish and soak in a large bowl of cold water for a minimum of 24 hours, changing the water at least four times. See page 64 for detailed instructions.

Remove the skin and large bones and cut into serving pieces before cooking. Drain well in a colander.

Heat the oil over low heat in a heavy saucepan with lid, and add the cayenne, stirring constantly for a few minutes to release its flavor. Take care that it doesn't burn. Add the onions and garlic and sauté lightly until soft. Stir in the tomato (or tomato paste) and add the potatoes and a few good grindings of black pepper. Pour in the water so that it almost covers the potatoes and simmer, covered, for about 10 minutes. Then place the salt cod pieces on top of the potatoes and simmer another 30 minutes until the sauce thickens. Sprinkle with chopped parsley before serving. *Serves 8.*

Salted Cod with Leeks

Bakaliáro me prássa

🏛 CORFU

1 salted cod (about 2 pounds/1 kg.)
2 pounds (1 kg.) leeks, washed
  and sliced
5 sticks of celery, finely chopped
1 cup (240 ml.) olive oil

freshly ground black pepper to taste
½ cup (120 ml.) water
2 eggs
4 tablespoons lemon juice

Soak the codfish in cold water and prepare as in the previous recipe. While draining, dry leeks and celery well. Heat the olive oil in a saucepan and add the leeks and celery. Sauté for 10 minutes, stirring so they don't burn. Season with pepper, add water, and simmer until the vegetables are soft and much of the water is absorbed. Place the pieces of fish on top of the vegetables and simmer, covered, 15 to 20 minutes, adding a bit more water but not more than another half cup. (The fish steams rather than boils.)

Remove from heat. Beat eggs and lemon juice together in a separate bowl—large enough to hold the cooking liquid. Pour the liquid slowly into the bowl and then return the contents to the saucepan, shaking it to distribute the liquid, and reheat gently without boiling. *Serves 6.*

Fish Stew

Bianco

🏛 CORFU

In Italian, a dish cooked in bianco simply means without tomatoes. This is a fine way to cook a delicate fish like a grey mullet, a bass, or, in the U.S., a striped bass.

3 pounds (1 ½ kg.) white fish
1 medium onion, finely chopped
1 head garlic, finely chopped
½ cup (120 ml.) olive oil
3 cups (720 ml.) water
½ teaspoon oregano

salt to taste
pepper to taste
6 or more medium-sized waxy
*   potatoes, peeled and sliced*
the juice of 1 lemon

If possible, buy the fish cleaned with the head(s) intact. They will make the stew thicker and tastier. Sprinkle the fish with salt (if desired) to firm the flesh and leave for 1 to 2 hours. Then rinse.

Place the onion, garlic, olive oil, water, oregano, salt, and pepper in a large shallow saucepan, and simmer for about 30 minutes. Add the potatoes and simmer 15 minutes more. Add the fish, which should be half covered by the liquid (add more water if necessary). Simmer 15 minutes, or until the liquid thickens and the fish is done. Stir in the lemon juice and serve with a salad and fresh bread. *Serves 6.*

Variation:
As a variation, you could sauté the onion, garlic, and sliced potatoes gently for 10 minutes before adding the water and seasonings.

Fish Stew from Paxos

Bourdétto Paxón

🏛 PAXOS

Paxos and Antípaxos (referred to in Greek in the plural, Paxí) are delightful small islands south of Corfu. Paxos has three villages; its main port is hidden at the back of a fjord-like channel and boasts one splendid mansion from the years of the British Protectorate. The islands were "discovered" in the late 1960s by yachtsmen and reporters on the trail of Jackie and Aristotle Onassis, who were sailing on the *Christina* to Skorpiós, his island off Lefkada. Their limestone cliffs, coast-to-coast olive groves, and tropical beaches tempted many sailors to linger. The islands have always been considered an appendage of Corfu, sharing their larger neighbor's fate.

This *bourdétto* with its accent on onions resembles a *stifádo*, a stew usually made with meat or hare.

3 pounds (1–1½ kg.) fish, grey mullet or sea bream

salt to taste

1 pound (½ kg.) large onions, finely chopped

1 cup (240 ml.) olive oil

3 cloves garlic, finely chopped

2 tablespoons tomato paste, diluted with 1 cup (240 ml.) water

2 tablespoons paprika or 1 tablespoon cayenne pepper

½ teaspoon freshly ground black pepper

2 pounds (1 kg.) small stewing onions

1 pound (½ kg.) potatoes, sliced in thin rounds

2 tablespoons chopped parsley

Wash the cleaned fish and sprinkle with salt. Sauté the chopped onions in half the olive oil for about 10 minutes until soft. Then add the garlic, tomato paste, water, and red and black pepper, and simmer for half an hour. Heat the rest of the olive oil in a separate pan and brown the small stewing onions. Add the onions, fish, and potatoes to the sauce and simmer for about 20 minutes. Serve sprinkled with chopped parsley. *Serves 6.*

Fish Kythera Style

Kythiriótiko psári

🏛 KYTHERA

In 1682, George Wheler was a bit disappointed when he arrived at the birth-place of Aphrodite. "Cerigo—anciently Cithaera—is famous for being the Native country of Venus and Helena: So that were we to frame an Idea of this place from the fame of those Beauties, we might imagine it one of the most charming places in the World. But on the contrary, the greatest part of it is a barren, rocky and mountainous Soil, ill peopled, and can brag of no plenty, nei-ther of Corn, Wine, nor Oyl: which undoubtedly made Venus change her own Country for Cyprus. . . ."

But it does have an abundance of fish.

3–4 pounds (1¹/₂–2 kg.) grouper or
    another large fish suitable for slicing
¹/₂ cup (120 ml.) olive oil
salt to taste
pepper to taste
1 pound (¹/₂ kg.) onions, finely chopped
1 tablespoon tomato paste
1 cup (240 ml.) white wine

2 cloves garlic, finely chopped
1 tablespoon parsley, finely chopped
2 pounds (1 kg.) tomatoes, ripe but
    firm, sliced [or a 16-ounce (400 g.)
    can of peeled tomatoes]
¹/₂ cup (50 g.) dry breadcrumbs
lemon slices

Have the fishmonger clean and slice fish into serving pieces.

Preheat the oven to 375° F. (190° C.). Wash the fish pieces and leave to drain in a colander. Place half the oil in a baking dish and lay the fish slices on top. Sprinkle with salt, pepper, and onion. Then dis-solve the tomato paste in the wine and pour it over the fish. Mix together the garlic and parsley, and sprinkle half the mixture over the fish. Place the tomato slices on top. Sprinkle the rest of the chopped parsley and garlic, this time with the bread crumbs added, over the tomatoes. Drizzle the remaining olive oil over the pan, and bake for about 30 minutes or until the fish is done. Serve garnished with lemon slices. *Serves 6 to 8.*

Fish Baked in the Oven with Wine

Psári sto foúrno krassáto

🏛 KYTHERA

It seems that the Kytherans have been fond of fish since time immemorial, judging from this quote from Beeton's *Book of Household Management* (1861): "So infatuated were many of the Greek gastronomes with the love of fish, that some of them would have preferred death from indigestion to the relinquishment of the precious dainties which a few of the species supplied them. Philoxenes of Cythera was one of these. On being informed by his physician that he was going to die of indigestion, on account of the quantity he was consuming of a delicious fish, 'Be it so,' he calmly observed, 'but before I die, let me finish the remainder.'"

1 large fish, whole (sea bream, sea or striped bass, red snapper) (3–4 pounds/1½–2 kg.)
1 medium onion, sliced
1 medium carrot, sliced
3 celery stalks, chopped
2–3 tablespoons butter, melted

1 cup (240 ml.) red wine or white if you prefer
salt and pepper to taste
2 teaspoons thyme
lemon slices for garnish
2 teaspoons parsley, finely chopped

Have the fishmonger gut and scale the fish, leaving the head intact.

Preheat the oven to 375° F. (190° C.). Sauté the onion, carrot, and celery in the butter for about 5 minutes to soften them. Place the fish in a buttered baking pan. Sprinkle the fish with the sautéed vegetables and their cooking juices. Sprinkle with the wine, salt, pepper, and thyme. Bake for about 45 minutes or until fish flakes easily with a fork. Serve garnished with lemon quarters and sprinkled with parsley. *Serves 4 to 6.*

Bourdetto with Grey Mullet

Bourdétto me kéfalo

🏛 CORFU

This is a variation of the salt cod recipe, using fresh fish—any white fish with few bones will do—leaving out the potatoes, garlic, and parsley. It is so simple, it is easy to see its origins as a fishermen's soup.

*2–3 pounds (1–1½ kg.) grey mullet
or any firm, white fleshed fish
salt to taste
½ cup (120 ml.) olive oil
2 medium onions, finely chopped*

*1 level tablespoon cayenne pepper
1 tablespoon tomato paste, diluted
with 1 cup (240 ml.) water
1 teaspoon thyme*

Have the fish scaled and gutted. Wash, sprinkle with salt, and leave the fish for 30 minutes (or even overnight) in the fridge.

In a large shallow saucepan, heat the olive oil, add the onions and cayenne, and sauté gently for about 5 minutes before adding the diluted tomato paste. Place a little thyme inside the fish and lay side by side in the saucepan. If the fish is too large, cut it in half. Cook over a low flame for about 30 minutes. Remove the fish very carefully to a platter and serve the cooking liquid separately. This dish is also excellent cold and left in its liquid, which will jell in the refrigerator. *Serves 6.*

Octopus Ragout

Ktapódi yachní

🏛 CORFU

Octopus, the poor man's lobster, really is almost as good and as delicate in flavor as the highly prized crustacean. All over Greece you see them hanging out to dry—from clotheslines or over railings—before being grilled over charcoal. In Corfu a stew of octopus and rice was eaten at engagement parties so that the family would prosper like the grains of rice and multiply in all directions like the creature's tentacles. This stew, however, has no symbolic significance.

3 pounds (1½ kg.) octopus, cut into
chunks
½ cup (120 ml.) olive oil
2 large or 4 medium onions, sliced
4-5 cloves garlic, finely chopped
3 bay leaves

1 tablespoon oregano
red or black pepper to taste
5 or 6 small potatoes per person
1–2 tablespoons tomato paste, diluted
in 1 cup of hot water

Place octopus pieces in a nonstick saucepan without water and simmer, covered. They will exude quite a bit of liquid, especially if they have been deep frozen. Discard this liquid; it will make the dish unnecessarily hard on delicate digestive systems. Return to the stove, adding the olive oil, onions, garlic, bay leaves, oregano, pepper, and onions. Sauté all together for a few minutes and just when the bits begin to stick, add 4 cups of water. Simmer partly covered until a fork pierces the octopus flesh easily. Then add the potatoes together with the tomato paste and boil uncovered until the sauce has thickened and potatoes are done. The potatoes turn a lovely warm red and taste at least as delicious as the octopus. *Serves at least 6.*

Squid with Rice

Kalamarákia me rísi

🏛 ZAKYNTHOS

1 medium onion, finely chopped
4 tablespoons olive oil
2 pounds (1 kg.) squid, cut into
bite-sized pieces
2 cups (450 g.) long grain rice
1 16-ounce can tomatoes, chopped
1¾ cups (360 ml.) water (or half
wine/half water)

2–3 sprigs rosemary
1 teaspoon or more sugar
salt to taste
freshly ground black pepper to taste
tabasco to taste (optional)

Sauté the onion in the olive oil in a large saucepan. Next add the squid and sauté a few minutes. Then pour in the rice, stirring to coat with oil before adding the rest of the ingredients. Cover and simmer until the liquid has been absorbed—about 20 minutes. Serve hot, warm, or cold. *Serves 6.*

Cuttlefish with Celery

Soupiés me sélino

🏛 CEPHALONIA

The cuttlefish is a tender-fleshed creature with a sweeter, more delicate taste than either squid or octopus.

2 pounds (1 kg.) celery, including
    leaves and stalks, roughly chopped
2 pounds (1 kg.) cuttlefish, washed
    and cut into bite-sized pieces, ink
    sacs reserved
2 medium onions, finely chopped
2 tablespoons olive oil
2 tablespoons butter

1 cup (240 ml.) white or red wine
3 cloves garlic, finely chopped
3/4 cup (180 ml.) tomato juice
2 tablespoons dill, finely chopped
pepper to taste
1/4 teaspoon sugar
salt to taste

Parboil celery in a little water for about 10 minutes, drain, and set aside. Place cuttlefish in a nonstick saucepan and simmer for about 5 minutes. The cuttlefish will exude sufficient liquid to cook itself. Add the onion and simmer for another 5 minutes. Add the rest of the ingredients, including the ink from the ink sacs. Simmer until both cuttlefish and vegetables are tender and most of the liquid has evaporated. Season with pepper and sugar (and salt if necessary). *Serves 8.*

Seafood Casserole

Yiouvétsi me thalassiná

🏛 OTHONÍ

Othoní is one of three tiny islands—the so-called Diapontian islands—off the north coast of Corfu. Some historians think it could have been where Calypso held Odysseus enthralled.

Under the British occupation of the Ionians, it was a place of exile for rebellious islanders (mainly Cephalonians) pressing for union with Greece. Its population has dropped from about nine hundred to forty since the turn of the century, but inquisitive tourists are beginning to camp on its empty beaches.

This is a modern recipe.

¹/₄ pound (125 g.) butter [or 1 cup (240 ml.) olive oil]

1 head garlic, chopped

2 medium onions, chopped

¹/₂ pound (250 g.) mussels, cleaned and shelled

¹/₂ pound (250 g.) shrimp, cleaned and shelled

¹/₂ pound (250 g.) squid, cleaned and sliced

¹/₂ pound (250 g.) clams, shelled

4 ripe tomatoes, peeled and chopped (or 1 16-ounce can tomatoes, chopped)

1 teaspoon cayenne pepper

1 tablespoon tomato paste

2 chicken stock cubes

4 cups (1 liter) water

1 pound (¹/₂ kg.) package orzo pasta

4 tablespoons parsley

Heat the butter or oil in a large saucepan and sauté the garlic and onions in it for 2 or 3 minutes. Add the shellfish and sauté until they become opaque (do not overcook). Remove with a slotted spoon and set aside.

Add the tomatoes and cayenne pepper to the saucepan and cook over moderate heat until the tomatoes give up most of their liquid. Then dilute the tomato paste and stock cubes in the water and bring to a boil. Throw in the pasta, stirring every few minutes to prevent it from sticking together. Simmer until the pasta is soft, adding more water if necessary.

When the pasta is ready and the water absorbed, return the shellfish to the pan with a handful of chopped parsley, toss, and serve. *Serves 6 to 8.*

Mussels with Garlic

Mýdia me skórdo

🏛 ITHACA

This is the Ithacan version of *moules á la marinière*, which is also found on Lefkada. Clams would do just as well as mussels.

The Ithacans also used to make a pilaf with limpets collected from their rocky shores but no one can be bothered to gather them any more. The Lefkadians did the same with scallops, which they call *Capo Sante*, as do the Venetians.

4 pounds (2 kg.) mussels   2 tablespoons olive oil
5–10 cloves garlic

First, scrub the mussels well. Chop several cloves of garlic and sauté them in a little olive oil. Throw in the mussels when the garlic is soft and cover, shaking the pan occasionally. When the shells have opened, the mussels are done. Discard any shells that do not open. Serve them with some fresh bread for dunking and plenty of chilled white wine on some informal occasion. *Serves 6.*

CHICKEN AND OTHER BIRDS
(Kotópoulo kai álla pouliá)

Chicken, turkey, and game were staple foods of the middle and upper classes in the Ionian. Edward Lear, painter of watercolors and composer of limericks, used to complain bitterly of "dining on everlasting chicken" when he stayed in Corfu during the 1850s. He also frequently mentions the roads crowded with noisy turkeys on their way to be eaten. "The whole country is black with them and sounds of gobbling pervade the Corcyrean air." It was not unheard of to be served chicken twice during one meal, as John Davy discovered on an impromptu visit to a home in northern Corfu in 1835. The menu began with "rice and egg-lemon soup, followed by stewed foul in a savoury sauce and thin slices of bread soaking in it, roasted chickens, whiting and some other fish delicately fried, and lastly a dessert of almonds, melons, grapes and apple."

The islanders have numerous recipes for chicken. Because the chickens were apt to be free range (and a bit elderly), they have the habit of cooking them until the meat is falling off the bone and drenched in luscious juices. The Zakynthians had a few other tricks for tenderizing their turkeys. Apparently dousing them with a glass of rum or brandy before roasting helped, and they also resorted to the unusual practice of plunging the bird into salt water overnight—or even directly into the sea for a couple of hours—right after slaughtering.

Battery chickens (chickens raised factory-style) are really too tender for the long stewing that some of these recipes suggest. But with free-range chickens increasingly easy to find, you should be able to recapture the essence of these old recipes, and there is nothing tiresome about them.

Soula's Roast Chicken
Kotópoulo psitó
🏛 CORFU

Like most country women on the islands, Soula (Anastasia Spyrou) learned cooking from her grandmother. Her mother was usually too busy in the olive groves or doing other household tasks to do much in the kitchen. Recipes, such as this one, passed down through the generations have changed very little over time.

salt to taste

freshly ground black pepper to taste

2–3 bay leaves

3–4 cloves garlic, slivered, plus at least one head, cloves left whole

1 roasting chicken (2–3 pounds / 1–1½ kgs.), whole

2 lemons

1 small onion, halved

1–2 teaspoons oregano

1–2 tablespoons olive oil

1 pound (½ kg.) potatoes

1 cup (120 mL.) water

You can roast this chicken in a covered pot or in the oven. If the latter, preheat the oven to 325° F. (165° C.).

First, prepare a mixture of salt, pepper, crumbled bay leaf, and garlic slivers. Work this mixture under the skin of the breast, legs, and thighs. Make slits with a sharp knife in any parts you can't reach and slip a piece of bay leaf and a sliver of garlic into it.

Rub chicken all over with lemon juice and insert half an onion and half a lemon into the stomach cavity. Crumble some oregano over the chicken and drizzle a bit of olive oil over it as well.

Surround the chicken in the roasting pan with potato quarters—parboiled first for 10 minutes, if desired—whole garlic cloves (don't be stingy, there's nothing more succulent than roast garlic), and another lemon, quartered. Add a cup of water and roast for 2–3 hours until the meat is tender and the skin crispy. Turn once to brown the underside of the chicken and to make sure the potatoes cook evenly.

The chicken emerges crispy, fragrant with herbs, lemon, and garlic, and accompanied by a lemony gravy, made effortlessly. Even the lemon sections taste good.

Stewed Cockerel

Pastitsáda me kókkora

🏛 CORFU

A favorite Sunday/name-day lunch in Corfu is *pastitsáda*, pot roast in a rich tomato sauce served with macaroni. Some people like it even better when a cockerel is substituted for the beef. The cooking procedure is exactly the same whether you choose a well-aged, free-range bird or a piece of chuck.

1 hen or cockerel (3–4 pounds / 1 ½–2 kg.)	*1 tablespoon tomato paste, diluted in*
salt to taste	*the vinegar*
freshly ground black pepper to taste	*3–4 cloves*
1 teaspoon cinnamon	*sugar to taste (optional)*
3–4 cloves of garlic, sliced	*4 cups water*
3 tablespoons olive oil	*1 pound (½ kg.) package ziti or macaroni*
2 onions, sliced	*grated* kefalotýri, *Romano, or*
½ glass (120 ml.) good wine vinegar	myzíthra *cheese*

Before browning, make gashes in the bird and rub all over with a mixture of salt, pepper, and cinnamon, inserting the garlic slivers into the gashes. Heat olive oil in a heavy, lidded saucepan and brown the chicken thoroughly. Remove the chicken and cook the onion slices in the same oil until golden. Then stir in the vinegar and tomato paste. Return the chicken to the casserole with the cloves and a bit of sugar, if desired. Pour water halfway up the side of the chicken, bring to a boil, and cover. Then reduce the heat and simmer for 2–3 hours.

Check regularly to see if the water is evaporating too quickly, and turn chicken from time to time. Add more water if necessary, but do not dilute too much. You should have a thick sauce at the end.

As the serving time draws near, boil the pasta until al dente.

Cut the chicken into serving portions, pour sauce into sauceboat and serve with the macaroni, together with some thickly grated *kefalotýri* or dried *myzíthra* cheese. Or you can break with tradition and skip the macaroni, substituting crisp fried potatoes to soak up the rich sauce.

Stuffed Roasted Chicken

Kotópoulo psitó yemistó

🏛 ZAKYNTHOS

This recipe features the use of *ladotýri*, the island's hard piquant cheese whose flavor permeates the stuffing and keeps even the white meat moist.

1 chicken (2–3 pounds / 1–1 ½ kg.), plus the giblets

5 tablespoons olive oil

½ cup (120 ml.) white wine or light sherry (Zakynthians would use Verdea)

2 cups (100 g.) breadcrumbs from day-old bread

⅓ cup (50 g.) ladotýri, cut into small pieces (pecorino or another hard cheese would also do)

2 cloves garlic, finely chopped

2 teaspoons oregano

juice of 2 lemons

1 egg, beaten

freshly ground black pepper to taste

salt to taste (optional)

1 bay leaf

2 pounds (1 kg.) potatoes, peeled and quartered

Preheat oven to 370° F. (190° C.). Finely chop the giblets and sauté them in 2 tablespoons of the olive oil. Add the wine and simmer a little before adding the breadcrumbs, cheese, garlic, oregano, and juice of half a lemon. Stir well and heat through a further 2–3 minutes. The breadcrumbs will absorb all the liquid. Remove from the stove and cool before stirring in the egg. Season with pepper (the cheese may add enough salt).

Wash and dry the chicken. Sprinkle with salt and pepper inside and out, and place the bay leaf in the stomach cavity. Then stuff the chicken with the prepared mixture and place in roasting pan surrounded with the potatoes, sprinkled with salt and pepper if desired. Pour on the rest of the olive oil and the rest of the lemon juice. Roast in the preheated oven for about 1 ½ hours. *Serves 4 to 6.*

Chicken as Cooked in the Village of Agalá

Horiátiko kotópoulo apó ton Agalá

🏛 ZAKYNTHOS

Agalá is a small village in the northeast of Zakynthos. The village itself is not particularly pretty, but in the evening it is just a short walk to a spectacular view of the sunset. Every summer June, her husband, and assorted cousins make at least one expedition there to eat this chicken dish with mountains of *mezédes* and a dish of macaroni laced with sauce from the chicken. When the chicken itself finally arrives, they hardly have room for it. Accompanied by rather too many liters of delicious red wine, this is what one cousin calls "the full treatment."

This is one of the few dishes that tastes better made with tomato paste rather than fresh tomatoes.

1 chicken (3 pounds / 1 ½ kg.), cut in serving pieces, plus giblets, chopped	*2–3 bay leaves*
	3 cloves
¼ cup (60 ml.) olive oil	*1–2 heads garlic*
1 tablespoon tomato paste	*salt to taste*
1 cup water	*freshly ground black pepper to taste*
1 stick cinnamon	*sugar to taste (optional)*

In a frying pan sauté the chicken giblets in the olive oil for about 5 minutes and set aside. Sauté the chicken pieces in the same pan. Then transfer chicken and giblets to a larger saucepan, adding the tomato paste diluted in a cup of water and all the other seasonings, plus a little sugar if desired. Simmer slowly until the chicken is tender and the sauce has thickened. If necessary, add a little hot water from time to time. Serve with fresh bread to dunk in the delicious sauce. *Serves 4.*

Casserole Roasted Chicken
Kotópoulo in úmido
🏛 CORFU

The bilingual name of this recipe (*umido* is Italian for ragout) reflects its origins. The 87-year-old woman who gave it to Diana glowed with pleasure, remembering her excitement on her name day on the 15th of August when this steaming chicken would be brought in to the lunch table followed by a big bowl of mashed potatoes.

*1 roasting chicken (3 pounds /
    1 1/2 kg.), whole
3 tablespoons olive oil
1 glass white wine
1 pound (1/2 kg.) tomatoes, skinned,
    seeded, and grated*

*1 bay leaf
salt to taste
freshly ground black pepper to taste*

In a heavy saucepan or Dutch oven, brown chicken all over in olive oil. Remove and pour in the wine, scraping up any bits that have stuck to the pan. Return chicken to pan with tomatoes, bay leaf, and seasonings. Cover and simmer until done, adding more wine if necessary. *Serves 4 to 6.*

Stuffed Roasted Chicken
Kotópoulo psitó yemistó
🏛 CEPHALONIA

This recipe also calls for cheese, this time Parmesan, which with the olives and spices that gives it a rich, earthy taste.

*1 chicken (3 pounds / 1 1/2 kg.), with
    giblets, chopped
1/2 lemon for rubbing
salt to taste
freshly ground black pepper to taste
3 tablespoons butter
1 large head of garlic, peeled and chopped
2 teaspoons oregano*

*2 cloves
1 teaspoon ground cinnamon
1/4 cup (60 ml.) lemon juice
4 tablespoons dry breadcrumbs
1/2 cup black olives, pitted
1/2 cup (100 g.) Parmesan cheese,
    sliced as thinly as possible
1 egg, beaten*

Preheat oven to 375° F. (190° C.). Wash and dry the chicken, rub with lemon, sprinkle with salt and pepper, and set aside. Sauté the giblets in one tablespoon of butter and then add the garlic, oregano, cloves, cinnamon, and pepper, plus the lemon juice. Simmer until all of the liquid is absorbed. Remove from the stove; and add the dry breadcrumbs, olives, and cheese; and bind them with the beaten egg. Stuff the chicken with this mixture and truss or sew up. Dab the rest of the butter onto the skin and squeeze some more lemon juice over the bird. Roast in the preheated oven for about 1½ hours, basting from time to time. The juices will make a delicious gravy, from which you may wish to pour off the fat. *Serves 4 to 6.*

Ground Beef and Pine Nut Stuffing for Turkey

Yémisma yia galopóula (1)

🏛 CORFU

1 pound (½ kg.) ground beef	*3 tablespoons piqnolia (pine) nuts*
2 medium onions, chopped	*fresh bread crumbs from 2–3 slices*
2–3 tablespoons butter	*of bread (optional)*
1 cup (240 ml.) white wine	*salt to taste*
½ cup (100 g.) currants	*freshly ground black pepper to taste*

Sauté the ground beef and onions in butter until both are browned. Add the white wine and currants and simmer until most of the wine evaporates. Remove from the heat, add the pine nuts and, if desired, the breadcrumbs. Season with salt and pepper and let cool before stuffing the turkey. *Makes enough stuffing for a small (10–12 lb./5–6 kg.) turkey.*

Chestnut and Sausage Stuffing for Turkey

Yémisma yia galopoúla (2)

🏛 CORFU

1 pound (½ kg.) chestnuts, parboiled
and cleaned
1 cup (240 ml.) milk
1 pound (½ kg.) country sausage
(or sweet Italian sausage or pork
sausage meat), removed from its
casing and crumbled
2 medium onions, chopped

3 garlic cloves, finely chopped
2 tablespoons butter
½ cup (120 ml.) brandy
¼ teaspoon grated nutmeg, optional
3 tablespoons parsley, finely chopped
salt to taste
freshly ground black pepper to taste

After cleaning the chestnuts, simmer them with the milk for about 10 minutes. Remove them from the pan and chop them into small pieces. In a saucepan, sauté the sausage, onion, and garlic in the butter until the sausage is no longer pink and the onions are lightly browned. Add the brandy, chestnuts (and nutmeg if used), and simmer until most of the brandy has evaporated. Season with the parsley, salt, and pepper and let cool before stuffing the bird. *Makes enough stuffing for a 10–12 pound / 5–6 kg. turkey.*

GAME

(Kynígi)

In the old days, ammunition was scarce, so the islanders caught their game birds with snares and nets. It is a strange and picturesque sight to glimpse a country woman casting her net into the sky as if she were fishing.

Stuffed Partridge

Pérdikes yemistés

🏛 LEFKADA

2 partridges or Cornish game hens, giblets reserved
4 tablespoons olive oil
4 scallions, chopped
2 garlic cloves, chopped
4 tablespoons rice
8 tablespoons stock (made from the poultry necks or ¼ of a chicken stock cube)

2 tablespoons parsley, chopped
½ cup (50 g.) feta or kefalograviéra cheese crumbled
4 tablespoons of lemon juice
salt to taste
freshly ground black pepper to taste

Wash and dry the birds and set aside. Chop the giblets finely and sauté in 2 tablespoons of the olive oil until lightly browned. Add the scallions and garlic and continue sautéing. Add the rice, stirring until the grains turn opaque. Add the stock, stirring until the liquid is absorbed. Remove from heat and add the parsley and cheese, mixing well. When the stuffing is cool enough to handle, stuff the birds.

Heat the rest of the olive oil in a large saucepan and brown the birds in it. Next add the lemon juice, salt, pepper, and a little more stock or water, and cover. Simmer until the juices run yellow and a leg moves easily in its socket. Check from time to time, adding liquid if necessary to prevent sticking. *Serves 4.*

Partridge Pilaff

Pérðika piláfi

🏛 CEPHALONIA

Game-farm partridges or Rock Cornish game hens would be fine in this dish.

2 partridges, cleaned, washed,
    and halved
½ cup (120 ml.) olive oil
1 medium onion, finely chopped
1 tablespoon tomato paste, diluted in
    1 cup (240 ml.) water

5 cloves
salt to taste
freshly ground black pepper to taste
½ cup (250 g.) long grain rice

Dry the halves of the birds well. Heat the olive oil and brown them quickly all sides. Remove them and set aside. Sauté the onion in the remaining oil until soft. Return the browned birds to the pan adding diluted tomato paste. Season with cloves, salt, and pepper. Simmer until the flesh is nearly tender, adding hot water if necessary.

Make the pilaff: add water until there are about 2 cups of liquid in the saucepan, bring to the boil, and stir in the rice. Simmer covered until the rice has absorbed all the liquid (about 20 minutes). *Serves 4 to 6.*

Woodcock Salmi

Bekátsa salmí

🏛 CORFU

Gone are the days when we could say, as Edward Lear once did, that "woodcocks have become . . . so vulgar and common they are not presentable any more."

4 woodcocks (pigeon, partridge, or Rock Cornish game hens will do in the absence of these long-beaked birds), giblets reserved	1 tablespoon flour
	1 cup (480 ml.) water or stock
	2 bay leaves
freshly ground black pepper to taste	1 teaspoon black peppercorns
5 tablespoons butter or olive oil	4 tablespoons parsley, chopped
1 medium onion, very finely chopped	4 sprigs celery, chopped
1 cup (240 ml.) white wine	1 tablespoon tomato paste
3 tablespoons rusk crumbs (or dried bread crumbs)	salt to taste
	fried bread or toast, crusts removed and sliced in triangles

Sprinkle the birds with pepper and sauté in 2 tablespoons of the butter or oil until browned on all sides. Set aside to cool.

Meanwhile cut the giblets into small pieces. In another saucepan sauté the onion in the rest of the butter or oil until soft, then add the giblets and sauté five minutes more. Add ½ cup of wine, 2 tablespoons of the liquid from the sautéed birds, and the rusk crumbs. Stir over low heat until a thickish sauce results. Set aside.

Spoon off the oil from the sautéed birds and heat in a small saucepan. Add the flour and stir until brownish. Stir in the water or stock, adding the bay leaves, peppercorns, parsley, celery, tomato paste, and salt. Cut the birds into serving pieces and replace in the saucepan along with the sauce and the rest of the wine. Cover and let simmer until the birds are tender.

To serve spread a teaspoon of the heated giblet mixture over each slice of fried bread or toast, place on a platter with the birds on top, pour the sauce over them, and serve with pilaff or potato puree. *Serves 4 to 6.*

Pigeons with Broad Beans

Pitsoúnia me koukiá

🏛 OTHONI

If pigeons are not available, substitute quail, fresh or frozen, or Cornish game hens. A good alternative for the broad beans used here would be peas—which would need less cooking—Italian fava beans, or lima beans. This dish is delightful with a simple rice or bulgur pilaff.

3 tablespoons olive oil
4 garlic cloves or more, coarsely chopped
4 pigeons, whole
2 pounds (1 kg.) broad beans, fresh or frozen

2 tablespoons dill, chopped
½ cup (120 ml.) white wine
1 chicken stock cube or salt to taste
freshly ground black pepper to taste

Cover the bottom of a heavy saucepan with the oil, add the chopped garlic, and sauté for a few minutes. Then add the birds and brown them well on all sides, adding a little more oil if necessary.

If the broad beans are fresh, add them after 10 minutes of browning, then stir in the dill, white wine, seasonings, and enough water to almost cover the birds. (If you use peas or frozen beans, add them during the last 15 minutes of cooking.) Leave the birds to simmer slowly for 30 to 45 minutes until a leg can easily be separated from the body. (The Greeks love their meat and poultry very well done; you do not have to cook the birds so long if you prefer them otherwise.) If there is too much liquid, bring to the boil and let evaporate until you have the desired amount. *Serves 4.*

MEAT
(Kréas)

With so many days dedicated to fasting and with so much of the population poor for so long, meat has never been an important feature of the Ionian diet. Visitors in the nineteenth century complained about the butchers' scant offerings due to the long and frequent fasting periods. Nevertheless, there were restaurants in the towns where people could get a meaty meal—consisting largely of offal—very cheaply. Archduke Ludwig Salvator reports that in the early years of this century the Zakynthian workers used to breakfast on *patsás*, a stew of ox feet, bones, and tripe, along with bread and wine for 20 cents, while fried lamb's lungs, calf's liver, or *kokorétsi* (baked intestine stuffed with innards) cost a mere 5 pennies.

Meat, when it did exist, was very tasty. Kid and lamb fed on mountain herbs like thyme, marjoram, sage, and *rígani*, pigs on windfall olives. Cattle were in short supply, for all grazing land had been planted with currant vines or olive trees. But for special occasions, even beef (from a young steer) could be found. Most of the recipes included here would have been Sunday or name-day dishes, each location having its characteristic favorites. Most of them, too, require lengthy cooking, since meat in Greece is rarely aged long enough to become tender.

Veal with Garlic and Parsley

Sofrito

🏛 CORFU

This, together with *bourdétto* and *pastitsáda*, is the most famous dish from Corfu. It combines the islanders' two favorite flavorings, garlic and parsley, and the name betrays its Italian origins—*soffriggere* means to fry gently. *Sofrito* usually consists of finely chopped onion, parsley, celery, garlic, and carrot added to a stew or soup.

Don't buy the best cut of meat for this dish; it needs lengthy cooking to amalgamate all the ingredients into a thick, rich sauce that is a garlic lover's delight. In fact, veal is probably the wrong word for the meat used. In Italy, it would be *vitellone*, in Greece *moschári*—a young steer but well beyond the milk-fed stage.

Mashed potatoes are an excellent accompaniment.

2 pounds (1 kg.) beef or red veal
salt to taste
freshly ground black pepper to taste
flour
1 tablespoon butter or margarine

1–2 tablespoons olive oil
1 bunch broad leaved parsley, chopped
1 head garlic, slivered
1 cup (240 ml.) good quality white-
  wine vinegar

Get the butcher to cut 12 slices of rump steak and tell him to pound them as he would schnitzel—until they are about 3–4 inches wide and ¾ inch thick.

Have two plates ready, one containing salt and freshly ground black pepper on it, the other flour. Dust the meat slices quickly on both sides in the salt and pepper, and then in the flour. Make sure both sides of the meat are coated with flour, too.

Heat the butter (or margarine) with the oil in a nonstick pan and fry the meat slices very quickly, a few at a time, on each side to seal. Remove and set aside, until all are done.

Then take a large round saucepan with lid, place meat slices on the bottom, overlapping, and scatter a handful of parsley and garlic over them. Top with another layer of meat, parsley and garlic until all the meat slices in place.

Then add the wine vinegar to the pan, topping up with water to barely cover the meat. Bring to a boil quickly, then reduce heat, and simmer, covered, for at least one hour. Test with a fork for tenderness; the dish is done when the meat starts to fall apart. The consistency of the sauce should be thick. If it is too watery, boil down rapidly; if it is too thick add a little water.

The vinegar is essential; its pungency counteracts the sweetness of the garlic. *Serves 6.*

Zante Ragout
Sáltsa
🏛 ZAKYNTHOS

This is the Zakynthians' national dish. Unfortunately with the increase of tourism on the island, the local tavernas and restaurants have begun to skip the cheese, which is the vital part. Their excuse is that the tourists (Greek and foreign) would find the dish too rich. *Sáltsa* is delicious and can be served with fried or mashed potatoes, rice, or even as an appetizer with fresh bread and plenty of local Verdea or another white wine.

2 pounds (1 kg.) beef, cubed	sugar to taste
½ cup (120 ml.) olive oil	freshly ground black pepper to taste
2 pounds (1 kg.) ripe tomatoes, peeled, halved, and grated, or 1 tablespoon tomato paste	1 cup (100 g.) cheese, diced (preferably Zakynthos ladotýri but pecorino or another piquant cheese will do)
4 cloves garlic, minced	2 teaspoons oregano
2 bay leaves	salt to taste
4 cloves (optional)	

Dry the meat well. Brown it quickly on all sides in very hot oil. Then add the tomatoes, garlic, bay leaves, and cloves, if used, and season with sugar and pepper to taste. Simmer until the meat is tender and the sauce thickens. Just before serving stir in the cheese and the oregano. *Serves 6 to 8.*

Caution: add salt after the cheese, since the cheese is fairly salty.

Ragout of Beef or Veal
with Macaroni

Pastitsáda

🏛 CORFU

Pastissada is a Venetian word, and this recipe is very similar to dishes still served in the Veneto. The Corfiot version is famous throughout Greece.

2 pounds (1 kg.) lean beef or veal, cubed	1 stick cinnamon
1 pound (½ kg.) onions, finely chopped	1 tablespoon hot red pepper (optional)
½ cup (120 ml.) olive oil	½ teaspoon ground black pepper
2 tablespoons tomato paste	1 pound (½ kg.) package thick
1 cup (240 ml.) white wine	macaroni or bucatoni
1 head garlic, finely chopped	3 tablespoons butter
4–5 cloves	1 cup kefalotýri, Romano, or
3 bay leaves	Parmesan cheese, grated
1 tablespoon vinegar	

Sauté the meat and onion in the olive oil until lightly browned. Mix the tomato paste with the wine and pour over the meat. Add the rest of the ingredients except the macaroni, butter, and cheese. Simmer about 1½ hours until the meat is tender, adding a little hot water if necessary.

As the meat nears readiness, boil the macaroni in plenty of salted water until al dente and then drain. Place the macaroni on a large platter and sprinkle liberally with grated cheese. Heat the butter until sizzling and pour over the cheese. Serve the meat with its sauce in a separate bowl. *Serves 6 to 8.*

Variations:

Since this one of the best known of the Corfiot specialties there are, not surprisingly, many different claims to the "authentic" recipe. One version calls for a single piece of pot roast, studded with garlic and powdered cinnamon, browned with onions and deglazed with half a glass of vinegar. It also omits the hot pepper.

In another, you do not brown the meat at all but heat it in a covered, nonstick pan with some salt and pepper until it exudes its liquid and then simmer uncovered until it evaporates. Then you add the onions, garlic, bay leaves, cloves, cinnamon, and olive oil, and sauté stirring for about 10 minutes before adding the tomato paste and water.

Whichever method you choose, you'll end up with a very good dish.

Zakynthian Ragout of Beef or Veal with Macaroni

Ragoú me makarónia

🏛 ZAKYNTHOS

This, the Zakynthian version of *pastitsáda*, is a typical Sunday dish on the island. The pasta might be served as a first course, along with the sauce, then the meat would follow as a second course.

*2 pounds (1 kg.) beef or veal in one
    piece (preferably rib or sirloin)*
1/2 cup (120 ml.) olive oil
1 medium onion, grated
1 cup (240 ml.) wine (red or white)
*1 pound (1/2 kg.) ripe tomatoes,
    peeled, halved, seeded, and grated*
6 cloves
1 teaspoon whole black peppercorns

4 sticks cinnamon
3 bay leaves
a few whole allspice berries
1/2 nutmeg, grated
salt to taste
1 pound (1/2 kg.) ziti or macaroni
*1 cup kefalotýri, Romano, or
    Parmesan cheese, grated*

Dry the meat well. Heat the olive oil in a saucepan and sauté the grated onion for a few minutes before adding the meat. Brown it on every side and then add the wine, followed by the rest of the ingredients, except the pasta and cheese. The liquid should barely cover the meat; if it does not, add a little water. Simmer until the meat is tender and the sauce has thickened. Serve with very thick macaroni, tossed with some of the sauce and sprinkled with grated cheese. *Serves 6.*

Pot Roast Beef or Veal
with Parsley

Psitó maindanáto

🏛 CORFU

Here is another recipe that demonstrates the Corfiot passion for parsley.

*1 large bunch of Italian parsley, finely
    chopped*
2 medium onions, finely chopped
2–3 cloves garlic, finely chopped
¼ teaspoon powdered cloves
salt to taste
freshly ground black pepper to taste
*3 pounds (1½ kg.) beef or veal
    (rolled rib, rump, or another cut)*

2 tablespoons olive oil
2 tablespoons butter
*½ cup (120 ml.) sweet
    Mavrodáphne wine*
1 cup (240 ml.) hot water

Mix together the parsley, onions, garlic and powdered cloves, seasoning them with salt and pepper to taste. Make small incisions
about 1 inch long all over the meat and stuff each one with a little of
this mixture. Lightly brown the meat in the oil and butter. Add the
wine and hot water and simmer until tender, about 1 ½ hours. Add
more hot water from time to time if you see that the meat is in dan-
ger of sticking. *Serves 6 to 8.*

Baked Lamb with Rice and Yogurt

Arní sto foúrno me rísi kai yiaoúrti

🏛 CORFU

The yogurt in this dish indicates its mainland origins. Many of the people of Epirus across the sea were traditionally herdsmen and shepherds. Nineteenth-century English visitors reported that all of Corfu's meat came from Epirus and Albania.

2 pounds (1 kg.) lamb
4 tablespoons butter
2 cups (480 ml.) water
1 1/2 tablespoons oregano
1 cup (250 g.) short grain rice
salt to taste

freshly ground black pepper to taste
3 cups (600 g.) strained yogurt
(see page 66)
2 egg yolks, beaten
4 tablespoons flour

Preheat the oven to 375° F. (190° C.). Cut the lamb into small pieces about the size of walnuts. Dry them well and then place in a deep ovenproof dish with 1 tablespoon of the butter, the water, and the oregano. Bake for half an hour.

Remove from oven, pour the liquid into a saucepan, add the rice, salt, and pepper, and simmer for 12 minutes. Add more boiling water if necessary (the total amount of liquid should be equivalent to twice the amount of rice). Remove the rice from heat and let cool a little.

Meanwhile mix the yogurt with the egg yolks and flour until they are thoroughly blended. Stir the mixture into the rice and spoon it evenly on top of the lamb.

Dot with the remaining butter and cook in the oven at 275° F. (135° C.) for about 1 hour, until the yogurt sets. Just before serving, raise the temperature of the oven to 400° F. (205° C.) and cook until a brownish crust forms. *Serves 8.*

Roast Stuffed Belly of Pork

Pancetta yemistí sto foúrno

🏛 ZAKYNTHOS

June got this old recipe from a taverna in Zakynthos known all over the island for this dish.

3–4 tablespoons kefalotýri, Romano, or Parmesan cheese, grated
3 cloves garlic, finely chopped
1 smallish onion, finely chopped
1 teaspoon oregano
salt to taste

freshly ground black pepper to taste
2 pounds (1 kg.) pork belly
1 cup (240 ml.) white wine
juice of 2 or 3 lemons
1/2 cup (120 ml.) water
2 pounds (1 kg.) potatoes, quartered

Preheat oven to 375° F. (190° C.). Mix the cheese, garlic, onion, oregano, salt, and pepper together. Lay the meat out flat on a board and spread the mixture over it. Then roll the meat up and tie securely with string. Place the meat in a baking pan with the wine, lemon juice, and water. Surround with potato quarters. Roast in the oven for about 2 hours. *Serves 6.*

Stuffed Pork

Hirinó yemistó

🏛 CORFU

This is a specialty of the butchers of Corfu, who make it to order for their customers for parties of all sizes. Breast of veal can be substituted for the pork, if desired. This recipe is accented nicely by mashed potatoes.

1–2 medium-sized carrots
2 pounds (1 kg.) boneless pork, preferably shoulder
1 green pepper, roughly chopped
10 cloves garlic (less if preferred), chopped
4 tablespoons parsley, fine chopped

salt to taste
freshly ground black pepper to taste
2 tablespoons olive oil
1 cup (240 ml.) white wine or 1/2 cup (120 ml.) sherry
1/2 cup (120 ml.) water

Parboil the carrots and then chop them. Lay the pork out flat and place the carrots, green pepper, garlic, and parsley around in the center. Sprinkle with plenty of salt and pepper. Then roll up the meat and tie securely. Heat the olive oil in a saucepan and brown the meat on all sides. Douse with wine or sherry. Cover and simmer until tender, adding a little hot water from time to time if it starts to stick. Leave to cool a little before cutting into slices. The slices look very decorative with a mosaic of vegetables in their center. *Serves 6.*

Spiced Ham

Hiroméri

🏛 ZAKYNTHOS

The Zakynthians are the only Ionians left who make a kind of ham similar to prosciutto. The culinary tradition required making little incisions in the flesh, stuffing these with garlic, pepper, and cloves; covering it with coarse salt, and setting it aside for a few days. They would next scrape off the salt and put the

ham in a barrel full of brine to soak for three months. On Clean Monday they removed the ham from the barrel, washed it thoroughly in the sea (apparently it would be quite smelly), rinsed it with fresh water and then set it out to dry in the sun, so it would be ready around Easter. It still is a prominent feature of the Easter menu. Saltier than Italian prosciutto, the ham has a faint spicy flavor that is very pleasant. Sometimes it is boiled with Verdea wine, herbs, and bay leaves.

The Blue Grotto at Zakynthos

Meatballs

Polpéttes

🏛 ZAKYNTHOS

In Zakynthos, at least until the mid-1960s, *polpéttes* were indispensable fare for any picnic either on land or sea. They are still a favorite with tourists— under another guise as "hamburgers," and are taken on cruises to Smuggler's Bay, site of a famous wreck.

Homo sapien meets Caretta caretta

June can remember wonderful excursions to the uninhabited island of Marathoníssi (also a nesting ground for the endangered *Caretta caretta* sea turtles) opposite the now overcrowded beach of Laganá. The whole family would pile into a small caïque, with a canvas contraption to be erected on the island for shade, and a picnic consisting of plenty of sweet sun-warmed tomatoes, hunks of cheese, several loaves of crispy bread, mounds of *polpéttes*, bunches of grapes, an enormous watermelon, and, of course, a demijohn of Verdea wine and the obligatory bottle of olive oil. The watermelon was put in the sea to cool and water was drawn from the well.

On one such picnic the lunch had been stored by the ruined church and; while the party was exploring the island, some sheep appeared from nowhere and ate most of the food. Her English friends said it was the most memorable excursion they had ever been on.

3 slices stale bread, crust removed
2 pounds (1 kg.) ground beef or veal
1 teaspoon vinegar
1 egg
½ cup fresh mint, chopped or
*   1 tablespoon dried mint*

1–2 teaspoons oregano
4–5 cloves garlic, finely chopped
flour
olive oil (preferably)

Soak the bread in water and squeeze lightly. Mix with the meat, vinegar, egg, and spices and knead well. If you have time, leave the mixture covered in the refrigerator overnight to allow the flavors to blend. Shape the mixture into largish balls. Dip in flour and fry in olive oil. Serve hot or at room temperature. *Serves 6 to 8.*

If you want to avoid fried foods, then leave out the flour and bake them in a hot oven for about 10 to 15 minutes.

Meat Loaf
Polpettóne or Roló

🏛 CORFU

Another favorite with an Italian name, the secret of this meat loaf is that the meat must be kneaded and rekneaded, so that its seams can be really well sealed; otherwise it will crack open. This must be one of the few Corfiot recipes that calls for neither garlic nor onions.

½ loaf day-old Italian or Greek bread, crust removed	*freshly ground black pepper to taste*
2 pounds (1 kg.) ground beef (have the butcher grind it twice)	*3 tablespoons parsley, chopped*
	3–4 hard-boiled eggs
salt to taste	*flour*
	oil for browning

Soak the bread in water until it swells to twice its size. Then squeeze it as dry as possible and set aside.

Knead the ground beef very thoroughly, until it is very malleable. Add the bread, crumbled, and mix well again, this time with salt and pepper. Now flatten the mixture as you would a pie dough until it is about ½ inch thick and about 12 inches wide. Sprinkle the chopped parsley down the middle and lay the hard-boiled eggs on top of it. Then fold over the right-hand side of the meat to cover the eggs, trying to press the two sides together until you can't see where they join. Do the same with the left flap, pressing down at the ends as well as in the middle. The loaf should be about 4–5 inches in diameter.

Roll the loaf in flour and brown in hot oil in a large saucepan, turning it on all sides, even the ends. If it starts to open or crack, quickly roll it over to seal it.

Remove from pan and deglaze with a little water (it's better to have too little than too much—you can always add more later if you have to). Return meat to pan, cover and simmer for about 1 hour. Cool a bit before slicing. *Serves 8.*

Soula's Moussaka

Mousakás tis Soúlas

🏛 CORFU

Soula's recipe for moussaka—which might be called the Greek national dish—differs from most because she deglazes the pan used for frying the onions and ground meat with vinegar. She also adds a touch of cinnamon to the meat filling and a suspicion of ground cinnamon and cloves to the béchamel topping just before spreading it over the meat and eggplant base. (Though the addition of cheese makes the sauce Mornay, the Greeks always call it béchamel.)

3 pounds (1 ¹/₂ kg.) round eggplants, in salted ³/₄-inch (2 cm.) slices

olive oil

1 medium onion, finely chopped

1 pound (¹/₂ kg.) ground lamb or beef

1 tablespoon butter

2–3 tablespoons good wine vinegar

2 pounds (1 kg.) ripe tomatoes, peeled and chopped, or the equivalent canned tomatoes

¹/₂ teaspoon cinnamon

2 tablespoons parsley, finely chopped

BÉCHAMEL SAUCE

4 tablespoons butter

4 tablespoons flour

4 cups (960 ml.) hot milk

2 eggs, beaten

¹/₂ cup kefalotýri, Romano, or Parmesan cheese, grated

¹/₄ teaspoon powdered cloves

¹/₄ teaspoon cinnamon

TOPPING

¹/₄ cup (25 g.) kefalotýri, Romano, or Parmesan cheese, grated

¹/₄ cup (50 g.) dried breadcrumbs

Sprinkle the eggplant slices with salt and leave to drain for about 30 minutes. Wash off the salt and bitter liquid and dry. Then lightly brown the eggplant slices, a few at a time, in olive oil. Set aside when you have finished. (See tip about grilling eggplant on page 181.)

To make the meat layer, fry the chopped onion and ground meat together in 1 tablespoon of butter (or more if necessary). When the meat is browned and the onions soft, add the vinegar and stir well, scraping up any residues. Then add the chopped tomatoes, cover to make them exude their juice, uncover and cook rapidly until most of the liquid has evaporated. When nearly all of it has been absorbed, add the cinnamon and parsley and season to taste with salt and pepper.

To make the béchamel sauce, first melt the butter in a saucepan and add the flour, stirring constantly until amalgamated. Then add the milk all at once, off the fire, stirring with a wire whisk to get rid of the lumps. Return to low fire and when the sauce thickens, remove from heat and set aside for a little while to cool a bit. Then fold in the eggs, cheese, and spices and season with salt and pepper to taste.

Now take a deep baking pan (15 x 11 in./40 x 28 cm.), lining it first with a layer of eggplant, then the meat filling, followed by another layer of eggplant, and top with the béchamel. Sprinkle more grated cheese and a handful of breadcrumbs over the surface, dot with butter and bake for 1 hour in a moderate oven, 375° F. (190° C.).

Cool a little before cutting in square serving portions. *Serves 10.*

Meat and Rice Croquettes
Krokéttes
🏛 ITHACA

This is a wonderfully economical way to make meat go further. It makes a light summer meal served with a green salad.

1 cup (225 g.) rice, boiled until very soft	salt to taste
1 pound (½ kg.) ground beef or veal (or even leftovers from a roast)	freshly ground black pepper to taste flour
1 cup (90 g.) kefalotýri, Romano, or Parmesan cheese, grated	2 eggs, beaten 4 tablespoons rusk crumbs
4 tablespoons parsley, finely chopped	olive oil for frying

Mix the rice, meat, cheese, and seasonings together. Form the mixture into croquettes. Roll the croquettes first in flour, then in the beaten egg, then in rusk crumbs, and fry in olive oil until golden brown and crunchy. These are good either plain or with a tomato sauce. *Serves 6.*

Glorified Cottage Pie

Paté me kimá

🏛 ITHACA

Found in an old notebook, this recipe surely dates from the British. It has been raised to new heights by being christened "pâté."

3 pounds (1 ½ kg.) potatoes
2 eggs, beaten
1 cup (90 g.) kefalotýri, Romano,
*   or Parmesan cheese, grated*
salt to taste
freshly ground black pepper to taste

1 medium onion, finely chopped
5 tablespoons butter
1 pound (½ kg.) ground beef
½ cup (120 ml.) white wine
3 tablespoons parsley, finely chopped
rusk crumbs

Preheat oven to 375° F. (190° C.). Boil the potatoes, drain, and mash well into a puree. When they have cooled a little, add the eggs and half the cheese. Season with salt and pepper, and set aside.

Sauté the onion in 3 tablespoons of the butter until wilted, and then add the ground meat and brown well. Douse with the wine, add the parsley, and simmer until the liquid has evaporated. Season with salt and pepper.

Butter an ovenproof dish and sprinkle with rusk crumbs. Spread half the potato puree in the bottom and spread the ground meat mixture on top of it. Cover with the rest of the potato puree. Melt the remaining butter and pour it over the potato topping. Sprinkle with the rest of the cheese.

Bake for about 40 minutes until nicely browned on top.

Ragout of Hare

Stifádo apo lagó

🏛 CEPHALONIA

The fact that there are so many recipes for rabbit and hare from the Ionian Islands no doubt reflects a plethora of game but also many hard times. Though beef, chicken, or lamb were considered luxuries, a hare could be trapped or shot with a fair amount of ease. Nowadays, hare are rarely encountered, so rabbit has been substituted. If you wish to use a hare, bear in mind that it's a much bigger animal and requires a longer cooking time.

In this dish the hare is browned and then marinated before being stewed in its marinade. The result is spicy and marries well with mashed potatoes to which grated *kefalotýri* or Parmesan has been added. It tastes like a good Provençal daube.

*1 hare (or rabbit), 2–3 pounds /
    1 1/2 kg., cut in serving pieces*
1/4 cup (60 ml.) olive oil
1 cup (240 ml.) red wine vinegar
1 cup (240 ml.) red wine
4 bay leaves
1 teaspoon oregano
1 teaspoon thyme
1 stick celery
2 tablespoons parsley, minced
1 carrot, sliced
1 medium onion, sliced

1 head garlic, chopped
15 black peppercorns
1 teaspoon ground cinnamon
3 cloves
1/2 teaspoon ground nutmeg
1 teaspoon dried mint
1 teaspoon dried basil
*3 medium-sized ripe or canned
    tomatoes, finely chopped*
salt to taste
1/2 cup (120 ml.) brandy

Dry the hare or rabbit well and sauté in hot oil until browned. Place the meat and the oil in an earthenware, ovenproof casserole dish and add all the rest of the ingredients, except the brandy. Leave to marinate in the fridge for at least 24 hours (2 days would be even better). When you remove it from the fridge, add the brandy, bring to the boil and then simmer for about 1 1/2 hours until the meat is tender. *Serves 6.*

Cephalonian Ragout

Lagotó

🏛 CEPHALONIA

Traditionally, this dish is made with hare cut into serving pieces and marinated overnight in wine and black peppercorns, but in the absence of hare, rabbit, lamb, or even chicken are often substituted. This dish also calls for tomato paste, though some people (including us) prefer it with fresh tomatoes. It is very unusual in that it contains both lemon juice and tomatoes. In Greek cuisine either egg-lemon or tomato sauces are common, but lemon, other than a few drops, is practically never added to tomatoes. The garlic, rather than being excessive, simply melts into the sauce, giving it a delightful aroma and consistency.

2 pounds (1 kg.) meat (hare, rabbit,
    chicken, leg of lamb, or kid),
    cut into serving pieces
3 tablespoons olive oil
2 heads garlic, unpeeled

1 tablespoon tomato paste, plus 2 cups
    of tomato juice or 1 pound
    (¹/₂ kg.) ripe tomatoes, pureed
salt to taste
freshly ground black pepper to taste
5 tablespoons lemon juice

Brown the meat in the olive oil and set aside. Boil the garlic heads until soft and squeeze out the garlic pulp. Place the garlic in a saucepan with the meat and the tomato paste diluted in the tomato juice or the pureed tomatoes. Season with salt and pepper to taste and simmer until the meat is tender and the sauce has thickened. Stir in the lemon juice. Serve with fried or mashed potatoes. *Serves 6.*

Rabbit with Garlic

Kounéli me skórdo

🏛 CEPHALONIA

The original recipe called for 5 heads of garlic and even we balked. But, in fact, we shouldn't have. The garlic just imparts a sweetness to the stew and thickens the sauce.

1 rabbit weighing about 3 pounds (1½ kg.), cut in serving pieces
vinegar
3–4 heads of garlic, leave the cloves whole
¼ cup (60 ml.) olive oil
1 cup (240 ml.) white wine

1 tablespoon tomato paste
½ cup (120 ml.) water
3 medium-sized ripe tomatoes, peeled, seeded, and grated
salt to taste
freshly ground black pepper to taste
juice of 1 lemon (optional)

Soak the rabbit in a solution of half cold water and half vinegar for at least 3 hours. Drain and wipe the pieces well and then brown under the grill for about 5 minutes on each side. Meanwhile peel the garlic; the skins will come off easily if you dunk them in boiling water for a minute or less. Sauté the garlic cloves gently in the olive oil and then add the wine, tomato paste diluted in the water, fresh tomatoes, and salt and pepper. Simmer for about 20 minutes before adding the rabbit pieces and continue cooking over a low heat until the meat is tender. Before serving, if you want, sprinkle with a little lemon juice to bring out the flavor. *Serves 4.*

Hare or Rabbit Ragout

Ragoú apó lagó i kounéli

🏛 ZAKYNTHOS

1 hare or rabbit weighing about
*   2–3 pounds (1–1 1/2 kg.),*
*   cut in serving pieces*
vinegar
1/2 cup (120 ml.) olive oil
2 tablespoons tomato paste

1/2 cup (120 ml.) water
2 teaspoons black peppercorns, whole
8 cloves garlic, finely chopped
salt to taste
pinch of sugar (optional)
1/2 cup (100 g.) small black olives

Marinate the hare or rabbit in vinegar overnight. The next day remove and wash and dry well. Heat the olive oil in a heavy saucepan until smoking and then add the meat pieces and brown on all sides. Dilute the tomato paste in the water and add to the meat together with the peppercorns, garlic, salt, and optional sugar. Cover with more water and simmer until the meat is tender and the sauce has thickened. Stir in the olives and simmer a further 5 minutes. *Serves 6.*

Rabbit in the Oven with Potatoes

Kounéli sto foúrno me patátes

🏛 CORFU

1 large rabbit (3 pounds / 1 ½ kg.),
   cut in 8 pieces
juice of 2 lemons
juice of 2 oranges
8 cloves, powdered (¼ teaspoon)
4 cloves garlic, minced

salt to taste
freshly ground black pepper to taste
1 teaspoon ground cinnamon
olive oil
4 pounds (2 kg.) potatoes, quartered

Wash the rabbit pieces well and then place in a bowl with the lemon and orange juices. Leave for 3–4 hours. Preheat oven to 375° F. (190° C.). Then drain the rabbit but reserve the juice. Make an incision in each piece of rabbit and insert a pinch of powdered clove and some of the garlic. Dry the pieces well and sprinkle with salt, pepper, and cinnamon before browning them in olive oil. When browned, place in an ovenproof dish and set aside. Next brown the potatoes lightly in the same oil before putting them in the dish with the rabbit. Cover the meat and potatoes with the reserved juices and bake for about 1 ½ hours. *Serves 6 to 8.*

Lamb Innards with Egg-Lemon Sauce

Sgatzétto

🏛 ZAKYNTHOS

While in the rest of Greece the Lenten fast is broken with a rich soup (*mageirít-sa*) made of lamb innards and scallions, this Zakynthos version is thicker and has more ingredients. It is eaten after the midnight service on Easter Saturday. Since many of these ingredients cannot be found in the U.S., you'll have to approximate the taste with liver and whatever else may be available. In any case, we would not have expected many American cooks to feel brave enough to tackle the cleaning of the intestines, but anyone who has eaten and enjoyed *mageirítsa* knows that the result is soothing and delicious. And this version is even richer. In Corfu, the ritual dish for Easter Eve is called *tsilíkourda* and is sometimes flavored with tomatoes instead of lemon.

innards of one lamb (liver, spleen, lungs, tripe, heart, sweetbreads, intestines)	*1 bunch dill, finely chopped*
	1 cup (225 g.) butter
	salt to taste
4 lamb's feet	*freshly ground black pepper to taste*
6 bunches Italian parsley	*2 cups (480 ml.) water*
1 veil of lamb	*3 eggs, separated*
6 scallions, finely chopped	*juice of 2 lemons*

Clean the innards and feet well. To clean the intestines properly, you should turn them inside out and hold them under the cold water tap. Take a lamb's foot and a bunch of parsley and wrap some intestine around it—repeat with the other feet and the sweetbreads. Place these in the bottom of a large saucepan. Wrap the remaining intestines around the veil of lamb and place it in the saucepan. Then sprinkle the rest of the innards, diced, over the top together with the scallions, dill, butter, salt, and pepper. Add 2 cups of water and simmer slowly, adding more hot water as necessary. *Sgatzétto* is more like a thick soup than a stew.

Just before serving, beat the egg whites in a medium-sized bowl until stiff and fold in the egg yolks and lemon juice. Add two or three ladlefuls of liquid from the soup, stirring slowly but constantly. Pour the contents of the bowl slowly back into the saucepan, which you have removed from the heat, stirring all the time. Serve at once. (Do not bring back to a boil.) *Serves 8 to 10.*

MEAT AND VEGETABLE PIES
(*Píttes me Kréas kai me Hórta*)

While Greece is famous for its pies of all kinds—cheese, spinach, custard, and others—made with paper thin *fyllo* pastry, the Ionian Islands, particularly Cephalonia and Ithaca, have evolved a series of savory pie dishes made with a heavier crust made of flour, olive oil, and often wine. A very elaborate version, known as *Venetziániko pastítsio*, is a holiday dish on all the islands and may be their ultimate ancestor. This is not to say that you won't find *fyllo* crust among these recipes, but it is not as typical.

Some of the recipes that follow could be made as individual pies. One can envisage the Ionian farmer or shepherd taking a hefty slice of a family-size pie out into the fields. It would have been a comforting snack.

Leek Pie
Prassópitta
🏛 CEPHALONIA

2 pounds (1 kg.) leeks, sliced
4 eggs
¹/₂ pound (250 g.) feta, crumbled
salt to taste
freshly ground black pepper to taste

PASTRY
See basic recipe on page 82 and cut
proportions in half.

Mix the pastry ingredients together until you can form a dough ball, wrap in foil, and set aside in the fridge. Boil the leeks in water for 10 minutes, drain, and leave in a colander for a couple of hours to dry.

Preheat oven to 375° F. (190° C.). Mix the leeks with the eggs, cheese, salt, and pepper. Remove the dough from the fridge and roll out 2 sheets of pastry. Place 1 sheet on a well-oiled round baking tin or pie pan (10 in./25 cm. in diameter), brush with olive oil, and spread the leek mixture on top. Cover with the other sheet of pastry, turning the edges in to make a border and seal. Slit a few vents in the top and then brush it liberally with olive oil. Bake for about 30 minutes. *Serves 6.*

Soula's Squash Pie
Kolokithópitta
🏛 CORFU

In Corfu, the squash used to make this pie is like a pumpkin—very large, roundish, but pale grey with pink-orange flecks. It's almost too pretty to cut. In the local dialect, it is called *spoúrdo*. Unlike the American favorite, this is a savory pie and could be made with butternut, Hubbard squash, or zucchini, as well as a Halloween pumpkin.

about 2 pounds (1 kg.) pumpkin or
    squash, peeled, seeded, and grated

2 medium potatoes

1 large onion

salt (optional)

1 cup (100 g.) hard cheese (kefalotýri,
    Romano, or dried myzíthra), grated

2 eggs, beaten

2 tablespoons fresh mint, chopped, or
    1 tablespoon dried

2 tablespoons máratho (fennel
    leaves), chopped

2 tablespoons parsley, chopped

salt and pepper

2 tablespoons currants (optional)

1 package fyllo pastry

olive oil for brushing leaves

(See note about working with *fyllo* on page 60.)

Grate pumpkin into a colander and then grate potatoes and onion into it. Sprinkle with salt (if desired) and let stand for 30 minutes. Then squeeze out all the excess liquid with your hands, a fistful at a time, and put the grated vegetables in a large bowl. Mix well. Add the grated cheese and then stir the eggs, herbs, seasonings, and currants (if used) into the mixture, so they are well blended.

Line a medium-sized oiled baking pan with 5 sheets of *fyllo*, painting each leaf with olive oil. When they are in place, spread the filling over them and top with 5 more sheets, which you also brush with olive oil. Brush the top of the pie with a little more oil, score into serving portions and bake for about 40 minutes at 375° F. (190° C.).

If you can't be bothered to work with crust, this filling also makes a delicious flan. Just add about ¼ cup (60 ml.) of milk and 2 tablespoons of flour to the mixture, slide it into a oiled baking dish, and top with rusk or bread crumbs over which you drizzle a little olive oil.

This flan is also excellent cold the next day, maybe even better. *Serves 6 as a flan, 8 as a pie.*

Vegetable Pie

Hortópitta

🏛 ITHACA

The Ithacans traditionally eat this vegetable pie on Clean Monday, the first day of Lent; therefore, it contains no butter, eggs, or cheese.

2 pounds (1 kg.) mixed greens, e.g. chard, leeks, spinach, sorrel, dill, fennel

salt to taste

½ cup (120 ml.) olive oil

½ cup (115 g.) short grain rice, parboiled for 5 minutes

freshly ground black pepper to taste

PASTRY

See basic recipe on page 82.

Wash the greens well and leave to drain overnight. The next day slice them very finely and sprinkle them with salt. Leave for another half hour and then squeeze well to remove excess liquid. Mix the greens in a bowl with the olive oil and rice and season with pepper.

Preheat oven to 375° F. (190° C.). Roll out two rounds of pastry to fit a round baking tin, 12 inches (30 cm.) in diameter. Place one piece of pastry in the bottom of the well-oiled pan and spread the filling over it. Top with the other round of pastry and make a few slits in it. Fold the surplus pastry over the edges. Bake for one hour. *Serves 6 to 8.*

Octopus Pie

Oktopodópitta

🏛 CEPHALONIA

We could not help but include this most unusual recipe; in fact, we don't think we've ever seen a recipe for octopus pie anywhere else. The Cephalonians eat it on the third Sunday of Lent. If you do decide to attempt this, you could "dine out on it" for months to come.

2 pounds (1 kg.) fresh or frozen octopus

3 medium potatoes, cubed

⅓ cup (75 g.) short grain rice

2 pounds (1 kg.) pumpkin, squash,
    or zucchini, cubed

4 tablespoons parsley, finely chopped

2 cloves garlic, finely chopped

2 medium tomatoes, peeled, halved,
    and grated, or 2 canned tomatoes

1 medium onion, finely chopped

2 tablespoons dill, finely chopped

black pepper

a pinch of powdered cloves

a pinch of grated nutmeg

½–1 cup (120–240 ml.) olive oil

PASTRY

See basic recipe on page 82.

Preheat oven to 425° F. (220° C.). Put the octopus in a saucepan and heat covered until tender. It will generate its own juices and may not need any water. Cut into small pieces. Mix all the ingredients together. Use the basic pastry recipe on page 82. After you have assembled the ingredients and filled the pie, brush the crust liberally with a mixture of olive oil, beaten egg and milk. Make a few slits in the top. Bake for 20 minutes, then lower the heat to moderate (375° F./190° C.), and bake for another 40 minutes. *Serves 8 to 10.*

Venetian Pasticcio

Venetziániko pastítsio

🏛 ALL ISLANDS

This recipe is the nearest we have found to a truly Venetian dish. But perhaps it is Sicilian. Whatever its origins, it is remarkable how similar this "pie" is to the following description from *The Leopard* by Giuseppe Tomaso di Lampedusa. In her book on Sicilian cooking, *Pomp and Sustenance*, Mary Taylor Simeti says that it may have antecedents in Ancient Rome, Tuscany, and France.

"The Prince was too experienced to offer Sicilian guests... a dinner beginning with soup... But rumors of the barbaric foreign usage of serving an insipid liquid as first course had reached the notables of Donnafugata too insistently for them not to quiver with a slight residue of alarm. So when three lackeys in green gold and powder entered, each holding a great silver dish containing a towering macaroni pie, only four of the twenty at table avoided showing pleased surprise ... The burnished gold of the crusts, the fragrance of the sugar and cinnamon they exuded, were but preludes to the delights released from the interior when the knife broke the crust; first came a spice-laden haze, then chicken livers, hard-boiled eggs, sliced ham, chicken and truffles in masses of piping hot, glistening macaroni to which the meat juice gave an exquisite hue of suede."

This so-called Venetian pastitsio was always a great dish for festive occasions and is still today, with rusk crumbs sometimes making a crunchy substitute for the sweet crust, top and bottom. However, no single person has the same recipe and the ingredients seem to vary depending on what is available. It could almost be called a "kitchen sink pie," as you could put in game birds, different cuts of meat, chicken, ham, mortadella, little meatballs, hard-boiled eggs, and chicken livers along with the macaroni, which was the one thing everyone agreed should be there. Naturally, no precise amounts were ever cited but we have tried to provide a workable recipe.

First, the ingredients for the sweet pastry (*pasta frolla*).

1 pound (¹/₂ kg.) butter	*1 teaspoon baking powder*
2 pounds (1 kg.) flour	*4 egg yolks*
2 ¹/₂ tablespoons sugar	

First prepare the pastry. Rub the butter into the flour, then add the sugar and baking powder. Beat the egg yolks and add to the mixture.

Knead the ingredients until smooth but as little as possible, adding a little water if necessary to make a pliable dough. Set aside, wrapped in foil in the refrigerator, for about an hour.

FILLING

1 pound (¹/₂ kg.) macaroni, bucatini, or ziti

¹/₂ pounds (¹/₄ kg.) chicken livers, cut in small pieces

1 pound (¹/₂ kg.) ground beef

1 pound (¹/₂ kg.) lamb or pork, roasted with garlic, herbs, and wine (optional)

3 tablespoons olive oil

3 tablespoons butter

¹/₂ teaspoon cinnamon

¹/₄ teaspoon ground cloves

salt to taste

freshly ground black pepper to taste

¹/₂ cup (120 ml.) white wine

1 small chicken, pot-roasted with lemon juice and a little oil (optional)

¹/₂ cup (45 g.) kefalotýri, Romano, or Parmesan cheese, grated

¹/₄ pound (100 g.) diced ham

3 eggs, hard-boiled and halved

4 tablespoons chopped parsley

Now prepare the filling. Boil the macaroni until al dente and drain. Sauté the chicken livers and brown with the ground beef (if you are using it) in the oil and butter and then add the cinnamon, cloves, salt, pepper, and the wine. Simmer until much of the liquid has evaporated. Cube the chicken and meat (if you are using them), being careful to reserve all the juices. Then toss the macaroni with the meat juices and cheese in a bowl.

Preheat oven to 375° F. (190° C.). Now divide the dough into two balls and roll both pieces out until you have enough to line a deep cake tin or baking dish. Place one on the bottom of the tin, leaving a couple of inches to spare around the sides. Spread half of the macaroni mixture evenly on top of the pastry, then add the cubed meats, ham, livers and hard-boiled eggs. Sprinkle with chopped parsley. Cover with the rest of the macaroni and flatten it with a spatula. Place the rest of the pastry on top, crimp edges together, cut a few slits to let the air escape, and brush with milk. Bake for about 30 minutes, until the crust becomes golden. Since all the ingredients are already cooked, it is just necessary to heat them thoroughly and brown the crust. *Serves 8 to 10.*

Meat Pie

Kefallonitikí kreatópitta

🏛 CEPHALONIA

Recipes for *kreatópitta* in Cephalonia are like recipes for bouillabaisse in Marseille: each one is offered as the only truly authentic version handed down by a mythical grandmother. We have unearthed quite a few recipes. Some contain prunes, raisins, almonds, or pine nuts—ingredients that Cephalonians told us emphatically were not authentic. Nearly everyone insisted that marjoram is essential as is lamb or goat (actually castrated goat was the meat traditionally used). One person said it was better not to use rice, another that eggs should not be included. Eventually, it all boils down to a matter of taste.

In the old times, however, potatoes were anathema. When de Bosset, the Swiss deputy of the British commander in Cephalonia, tried to introduce the locals to the potato, he was opposed vehemently by two priests who declared that this was the very apple used by the serpent to seduce Adam and Eve in Paradise. In fact, this distrust was so deep that the Cephalonian farmers did not plant potatoes in great quantities until after the Second World War.

Then, and in some cases even today, this pie and other dishes requiring long cooking would have been baked in the *tserépa*, a portable clay oven. It has a high initial temperature, which falls gradually, releasing the essence of the spices and herbs to make a much more delicious concoction than a modern oven. Before the widespread use of the refrigerator, the cook would have left the combined ingredients to marinate in a *fanári*—an open box with a couple of shelves surrounded by fine netting which hung from the ceiling to foil insects and rodents. She would have prepared the dish in the evening, after the wasps had retired to their nests; enthusiastic carnivores, they would have been a nuisance while she was cutting the meat into small pieces and trimming it of fat and gristle.

Rolling pastry, sorting greens

THE FILLING

1 pound (¹/₂ kg.) lean lamb or kid,
with no gristle or skin
1 pound (¹/₂ kg.) lean beef or pork
with no gristle
¹/₄ cup short grain rice
1 medium onion, finely chopped
2 medium potatoes, cut in smallish
cubes
1 cup (90 g.) kefalotýri, Romano, or
Parmesan cheese, grated
2 teaspoons powdered cinnamon
4 teaspoons fresh marjoram, finely
chopped (or 2 teaspoons dried)
4 teaspoons parsley, finely chopped

1–3 cloves garlic, finely chopped
2 medium tomatoes, peeled, halved,
and grated, or 2 canned tomatoes
1 cup (240 ml.) meat stock
salt to taste
freshly ground black pepper to taste
2 tablespoons olive oil
¹/₂ cup (120 ml.) wine, red or white
corn flour or wheat flour
2 hard-boiled eggs, cut in quarters
mixture of olive oil, beaten egg, and milk
2 tablespoons butter

PASTRY
See basic recipe on page 82.

Cut the meat into tiny pieces (as big as the tips of your fingers), making sure that you remove any traces of fat and gristle; this and the bones can be used to make the stock. Mix all the ingredients, except the boiled eggs, stock, and butter, together. Refrigerate overnight, if possible.

Preheat oven to 425° F. (220° C.). To assemble the pie, liberally oil a shallow round tin, 12 inches (30 cm.) in diameter. Roll out ²/₃ of the pastry on a surface sprinkled with corn flour or wheat flour. A long thin rolling pin like a broom stick was traditionally and is still used for this purpose. Line the tin with this pastry and then spread the filling over it. Tuck the boiled egg sections into the mixture, then pour the stock over it and dot with the butter. Roll out the rest of the pastry and cover the pie with it, sealing the edges and making a few slits in the top. Brush liberally with a mixture of olive oil, beaten egg, and milk. Bake for 20 minutes and then lower the heat to moderate, 375° F. (190° C.) and bake for another 80 minutes. *Serves 10 to 12.*

Ithaca Meat Pie

Kreatópitta tis Ithákis

🏛 ITHACA

Although this recipe uses *fyllo* instead of pie dough, the filling is typically Ionian.

*3 pounds (1 1/2 kg.) lean lamb, kid,
    or pork, cubed
2 tablespoons butter
2 tablespoons olive oil
1 cup (240 ml.) white wine
1 tablespoon tomato paste diluted in
    1 cup (240 ml.) of water
1 medium potato, grated
1 medium onion, grated
5 cloves garlic, finely chopped
4 tablespoons parsley, finely chopped*

*2 tablespoons mint, finely chopped
salt to taste
freshly ground black pepper to taste
1 cup (225 g.) rice
1 cup (100 g.) kefalotýri, Romano,
    or feta cheese, grated
2 hard-boiled eggs, sliced
1 pound (1/2 kg.) fyllo pastry
olive oil to brush fyllo pastry with
    (about 1/2 cup or 120 ml.)*

Preheat oven to 375° F. (190° C.). Dry meat chunks well and then sauté in the butter and olive oil until lightly browned all over. Douse with the wine and add the diluted tomato paste. Next put in the grated potato, onion, garlic, parsley, and mint, season with salt and pepper, and simmer for 5 minutes before adding the rice. Pour the mixture into a bowl and leave to cool before stirring in the cheese and eggs. Layer the bottom of a round baking tin (diameter 12 in./30 cm.) with five sheets of *fyllo*, brushing each sheet liberally with olive oil before you put the next. Spread the meat/rice mixture on top and then lay the remaining *fyllo* sheets on top, again brushing each sheet with oil. Score the pie into serving pieces and bake for 1 1/2 hours. *Serves 10 to 12.*

Lefkada Meat Pie
Kreatópitta tis Lefkádas
🏛 LEFKADA

This recipe uses home-made *fyllo* pastry, which requires a lot of work. It can never be as thin as the commercial pastry, but if you attempt to make it, try to roll it out as thinly as possible. You only need 3 sheets on the bottom of the pie and 3 sheets on top. If you feel you can't cope with making this pastry, use store-bought *fyllo*.

1 onion, finely chopped
1 tablespoon butter
4 tablespoons olive oil
2 pounds (1 kg.) ground beef or veal
4 tablespoons parsley, finely chopped
1 teaspoon ground cinnamon
1 tablespoon tomato paste diluted in
   1 cup (240 ml.) of water
salt to taste

freshly ground black pepper to taste

PASTRY
1 cup (240 ml.) strained yogurt
   (see page 66)
1 cup (240 ml.) olive oil
1 egg
2 pounds (1 kg.) flour, approximately
olive oil to brush pastry with

Sauté the onion in the butter and olive oil. Add the meat and brown thoroughly. Add the parsley, cinnamon, diluted tomato paste, salt, and pepper, and simmer until liquid has evaporated. Leave to cool.

Preheat oven to 375° F. (190° C.). Mix the pastry ingredients together (there should be no need to add any water). Form into 6 equal balls and roll out 6 thin sheets. Oil a medium-sized baking tin. Place 3 sheets on the bottom of it, brushing each with oil before placing the next, and then spread the meat mixture on top. Place the remaining 3 pastry sheets on top, again brushing with oil, and pinch edges together to seal. Bake for about 1 hour. *Serves 8.*

Meat Pie

Kreatópitta Kerkýras

🏛 CORFU

Here is the Corfiot version of the Cephalonian pie. Until about 15 years ago, Corfu butter was the only fresh butter available in most Greek grocery stores.

2 pounds (1 kg.) cubed meat
   (½ pork and ½ veal or beef)
4 tablespoons butter
2 medium onions, finely chopped
4–5 cloves garlic, finely chopped
6 whole allspice berries
4 cloves
½ teaspoon powdered cinnamon
¼ teaspoon black pepper
1 cup (240 ml.) white wine plus
   ½ cup (120 ml.)

2 tablespoons tomato paste dissolved
   into 1 cup (240 ml.) beef stock
1 cup (225 g.) short grain rice
2 tablespoons chopped parsley
2 cups (180 g.) feta, crumbled
1 cup (90 g.) kefalotýri or Parmesan
   cheese, coarsely grated
4 eggs, hard-boiled

PASTRY
See basic recipe for short crust on page 82.

Preheat oven to 375° F. (190° C.). Brown the meat cubes in the butter together with the onions and garlic. Then add the allspice, cloves, cinnamon, and pepper, and douse with 1 cup of wine. Add the tomato paste dissolved in a cup of stock, mix well, and simmer for about 30 minutes. Set aside to cool a little and then add the rice, parsley, cheeses, and eggs, and mix thoroughly.

Roll the pastry into 2 pieces to fit a medium-sized baking tin. Line the tin with 1 piece, spread the filling over it, and top with second piece. Slit the crust with breathing vents. Brush with olive oil and sprinkle with cinnamon. Bake for about an hour. Halfway through the cooking time, sprinkle with ½ cup (120 ml.) of white wine. *Serves 6 to 8.*

VEGETABLE DISHES
(Lachaniká)

The cuisine of the Ionian Islands is filled with delicious and imaginative ways of preparing vegetables. Most of them became imaginative out of necessity, the population as a whole being extremely poor for centuries and unable to afford meat more than a few times a year. Until well into the 1950s, the people in the hill villages survived on vegetables, oil, olives, and corn bread. In some remote places, even salt was considered a luxury, to the point that each member of the family would sprinkle a few crystals of sea salt on their serving of boiled greens rather than pour a spoonful or two into the cooking water. The rare exceptions were salt cod at Christmas, lamb at Easter, a hen boiled in case of illness, and the odd hare or pigeon shot by the man of the house.

Because Ionian wealth came almost solely from the land, many of the families that lived in town had their country estate, where they would spend the summers. The children played with the children of the tenant farmers and ate the same food. In a way the vegetable dishes of the Ionian peasants can be compared to the "soul food" of African-Americans. More than merely nourishing, they evoke a host of associations and traditions. Even today the gentry in town will go out of their way to find a really delicious recipe for *ftohófago* (baked vegetables) like their nannies used to make, and all the islands have a multitude of cherished ways of cooking their greens.

The main thing that distinguishes Ionian vegetable dishes from those of the mainland is the lavish use of herbs. With the exception of hot pepper (which is mainly found in the Corfiot *bourdéttos*), cloves, and cinnamon, the Corfiots and other islanders rarely season their cooking with spices. Herbs are another matter, with parsley the favorite, followed by mint and *máratho* (wild fennel), and even occasionally basil, which Greeks generally regard as a holy plant (see page 196). And of course, lots of garlic.

Stuffed Artichokes

Angináres yemistés

🏛 CEPHALONIA

Stuffed artichokes are little known in Greece, though very popular in Italy. In spring they are so plentiful that most dishes dispense with the leaves and use only the bottoms or hearts. The addition of potatoes makes this a main course dish rather than an appetizer.

6 artichokes
2 tablespoons lemon juice
1 tablespoon flour
6 heaping teaspoons short grain rice
7 tablespoons olive oil
2 cloves garlic, finely chopped (fresh if you can find it)
3 tablespoons dill or fennel, finely chopped

3 tablespoons scallions, finely chopped
salt to taste
freshly ground black pepper to taste
1 pound (¹/₂ kg.) ripe tomatoes, skinned, seeded and grated or canned tomatoes
¹/₂ teaspoon sugar
12 or more small new potatoes, peeled (optional)

Cut the stalks off the artichokes so that they can stand upright in the saucepan. Remove 3 or 4 layers of the tough outer leaves and cut about 1 inch off the top of the artichoke. Scoop out the fuzzy choke with a teaspoon. You should have a decent-sized cavity to stuff. As you clean the artichokes, place them in a bowl of water with the lemon juice and flour to prevent them from discoloring. Remove the fibrous outer part of the stalks and place them in the bowl as well.

Mix together the rice, 3 tablespoons of the olive oil, the garlic, the dill or fennel, the scallions, and plenty of salt and pepper to taste. Drain the artichokes and stuff the cavities with this mixture. Place in a saucepan together with the stalks. In another saucepan simmer the tomatoes with the sugar and the rest of the olive oil for 5 minutes and then pour over the artichokes, adding water if necessary so that the liquid comes halfway up the sides of the artichokes. Simmer covered for about 1 hour. If potatoes are used, add them after the artichokes have been cooking for about 30 minutes. *Serves 6.*

Stewed Artichokes

Angináres kokkinistés

🏛 CORFU

12 artichokes (2 per person)

3 lemons, halved

4 heads of garlic (preferably fresh
   garlic if available, chopped)

4 scallions, chopped

1 bunch fresh dill, finely chopped,
   or 3 tablespoons dried

1 big bunch mint, finely chopped,
   or 2 tablespoons dried

1 cup (240 ml.) olive oil

salt to taste

cayenne pepper to taste

12 small new potatoes, peeled

1 tablespoon tomato paste, diluted in
   a little water

Clean the artichokes, removing the tough outer leaves and the chokes. If you're feeling lazy, just slice them in half and cut out the choke. Rub each cleaned artichoke with a lemon half and then soak in water to which lemon juice has been added so they won't blacken.

Chop the other vegetables and herbs finely and put them into a shallow pan with the olive oil. Sauté them along with a little salt and cayenne until soft. If the artichokes are very young and tender you can add them and the potatoes to the vegetable mixture; if not, cook them for about 10 minutes before adding the potatoes. Coat the artichokes with the olive oil and then pour the tomato paste and water over the vegetables, adding more water to half cover. Simmer covered, shaking the pan from time to time so they won't stick, until all the vegetables are tender. If you want to thicken the sauce, swirl in a tablespoon of flour mixed with water. *Serves 6.*

Soula's Eggplant Stuffed with Parsley and Cheese

Melitzánes yemistés me maindanó kai tyrí

🏛 CORFU

Soula is a short, solid woman from Kontókali on the coast just to the north of Corfu town. When she was growing up, Kontókali was country. Now it's a heavily built-up resort area and Soula and her family have moved inland, where they raise their own vegetables and chickens. She and her husband, Thódoros, have adopted an English woman in the neighborhood and help her with the cooking and gardening.

Soula has never read a cookbook. Everything she makes has been handed down to her from her grandmother and, to a lesser extent, her mother. She measures her ingredients with her eye and describes them in adjectives like some, a lot, a little, a touch. She gave Diana these recipes while cooking 3 at a time, boiling some Greek coffee, cleaning up the kitchen, and rattling off stories about her past, faster than a jackhammer breaking up a sidewalk.

We have tried to render her recipes (and others similarly acquired) with a bit more precision, but don't worry about being too meticulous.

For this simple and succulent dish, you will need several long, thin eggplants, at least 2 per person—don't be stingy. Like most vegetables cooked in olive oil, they are even better the next day, room temperature, never straight from the fridge.

8 eggplants
olive oil for sautéing
2 medium onions, chopped
1 bunch parsley, finely chopped

1 cup (¹/₄ pound / 90 g.) coarsely grated cheese, preferably kefalotýri *or* Romano
freshly ground black pepper to taste

Make 3 gashes down the length of each eggplant (4 if they are plump enough). Sauté them gently in olive oil. Remove and drain.

Sauté the chopped onion in the same oil until soft. Remove from heat and add 2 handfuls of chopped parsley and the grated cheese to the pan. Mix well, add pepper but no salt as the cheese is likely to be rather salty. Then force the mixture into the slits in the eggplants.

Place the eggplants in an oiled baking pan and sprinkle a bit more olive oil on top. Bake in a moderate, 375° F. (190° C.), oven for 30 to 45 minutes. *Serves 4.*

For a fancier dish, serve with an egg-lemon sauce. (See page 84.)

Eggplant Smothered in Garlic

Melitzánes skórdo stoúmbi

🏛 ZAKYNTHOS

To our mind this is the best eggplant dish of all. Though a simple recipe with few ingredients, it is extraordinarily delicious. We always make more than we think we need in order to have leftovers, but no matter how much we make, there is never any left.

4 pounds (2 kg.) large round eggplants, unpeeled and cut in 1-inch (2 ½ cm.) slices and salted
olive oil for frying or brushing
4 pounds (2 kg.) ripe tomatoes, peeled, halved, seeded, and grated or 2 pounds (1 kg.) canned tomatoes

salt to taste
freshly ground black pepper to taste
½ teaspoon sugar to taste
2–3 tablespoons vinegar or sweet red wine (preferably Mavrodaphne*)*
1 head garlic, peeled and finely chopped

Preheat oven to 375° F. (190° C.). Sprinkle the eggplant slices with salt and leave them in a colander for 40 minutes to 2 hours to shed some of their bitter liquid. Wash and dry the slices well. Heat about an inch (2 ½ cm.) of olive oil in a frying pan and gently fry the eggplant slices in batches, taking care not to brown them too much. Drain on absorbent paper.

In another saucepan simmer the tomatoes with the salt, pepper, and sugar until a thickish sauce forms. Stir in the vinegar or sweet red wine. Arrange the eggplant slices in layers in an ovenproof dish, sprinkling chopped garlic between each layer. When all the slices are arranged in the dish, pour the tomato sauce over them and cook in the oven for about 30 minutes or simmer on top of the stove for about 20 minutes. The dish should not be watery and is best served lukewarm. It goes well with fresh country bread, feta, and plenty of wine. *Serves 8.*

Tip: If you disapprove of the way the eggplant slices drink up your precious olive oil, instead of frying them brush each slice on both sides with a little oil and set under the grill until slightly brown, turning when necessary. And for a milder taste of garlic, simmer it along with the tomato sauce.

Broccoli Zakynthos Style
Brokolínes
🏛 ZAKYNTHOS

In Zakynthos, the broccoli has dark purple florets clustered on a emerald green stalk. Though broccoli is a native of the eastern Mediterranean and was prized by the Romans, this variety was first cultivated in Calabria in the seventeenth century. No doubt, the Venetians with their nose for delicacies discovered it and introduced it to the Ionian. It reached the U.S. in colonial times, but did not become popular until the 1930s. It still is, George Bush notwithstanding.

The Zakynthiots and Lefkadians eat boiled broccoli with oil and lemon dressing on Christmas Eve. There is probably no ritual significance to this custom, but the vegetable does happen to be at its best in December. They are lucky enough to buy it cleaned, in small bunches like asparagus. They also drink the *brokolózoumo* or broth, adding a squeeze of lemon, which turns the water from vivid green back to purple. Apparently, this broth is an even healthier tonic if left overnight.

GREENS AND LEAFY VEGETABLES

(Hórta)

The Ionians are inordinately fond of greens of all kinds. Even in today's more affluent society, townspeople and country people, young and old alike, usually have their main meal at midday and have a light supper of boiled greens and a few olives. Ideally, the greens are wild, picked that very day. The open-air markets in every town make it easy for the residents to indulge this habit. Mountains of greens of every sort are piled on stands, brimming over buckets and baskets—arugula (called *róka* in Greek, *roúka* in Corfiot, rocket in English, and rarely seen in mainland markets), mustard, dandelion, curly endive, *séskoulo* (Swiss chard), radicchio, and diverse wild untranslatable varieties. For many Corfiots, the following dish is among the best loved. It is called *tsigarélli* from a Greek word meaning to sauté.

Sautéed Greens

Tsigarélli

🏛 CORFU

Though you could use spinach or any other greens that happen to be available, our recipe calls for:

salt for boiling (optional)

2 pounds (1 kg.) séskoulo (or Swiss chard, or silver or spinach beet), cut in fine shreds

1 pound (½ kg.) curly endive, finely shredded

2 leeks, chopped (use scallions, if no leeks are available)

2 or more stalks fresh garlic, if available, or 3 cloves, dried, finely chopped

2–3 tablespoons olive oil

3–4 tablespoons fresh mint, chopped, or 2 tablespoons dried

3–4 tablespoons fresh dill, chopped, or 2 tablespoons dried

2 small potatoes, thinly sliced

2 tablespoons cayenne

freshly ground black pepper to taste

salt to taste

Bring some water to the boil in a pot big enough to hold the greens, add salt (if desired), the *séskoulo*, and the endive. When reduced in bulk after approximately 5 minutes, drain in a colander as you would spaghetti, but reserve some of the liquid.

Then gently sauté the leeks (and/or scallions), and garlic in olive oil until soft, add the parboiled greens, the mint, and the dill together with the sliced potatoes, and toss well. Moisten with some of the reserved liquid; add the cayenne, black pepper, and salt; stir; cover; and simmer for about 30 minutes until most of the liquid has been absorbed. Check from time to time to see that the vegetables don't stick, adding more water if necessary. *Serves 6.*

Swiss Chard Ragout
Séskala Yiachní
🏛 ZAKYNTHOS

The Zakynthians love "séskala" (Greek *séskoulo*), their word for spinach beet or silver beet. It looks like a wild form of Swiss chard. They prefer it simply boiled with some *sélino* (pungent Greek celery) to give it more taste, drained and drenched with olive oil and lemon juice. This recipe is from the mountains, where it grows. There they parboil the *séskala* first in order to reduce its astringency. If you're using chard or beet greens, you could omit this step.

1 medium onion, chopped	*2 pounds (1 kg.) Swiss chard or other*
¼ cup (60 mL.) olive oil	*greens, boiled, drained, and chopped*
1 pound (½ kg.) tomatoes, peeled,	*salt to taste*
halved, and grated, or canned	*freshly ground black pepper to taste*

Sauté the onion in the olive oil and then add the tomatoes. Cook together for about 5 minutes before adding the chard or greens and cook slowly until the liquid is substantially reduced and thicker (about 20 minutes). Season with salt and pepper. If you add the chopped greens without parboiling them first, you may have to add a little water along with the tomatoes. *Serves 4.*

Ithacan Greens
Tsigarisména hórta

🏛 ITHACA

If the Ithacans have any left over boiled greens, they doctor them the next day by squeezing all the water out of them. Then they chop several stalks of fresh garlic and sauté them lightly in olive oil. When the garlic has softened they throw in the greens, heat them thoroughly and serve them sprinkled with vinegar.

Green Vegetable Stew
Láchano bourdétto

🏛 CORFU

This is another version of *tsigarélli*, but the vegetables are sautéed before any liquid is added to them. Both are equally good. Though on the mainland, *láchano* means cabbage, it simply means vegetable in Corfiot. The Corfiot word for cabbage is *"krabí,"* the Ithacan is *"máppa."*

½ cup (120 ml.) olive oil
1 pound (½ kg.) cabbage, thinly sliced
½ pound (¼ kg.) beet greens or
　　Swiss chard
4 tablespoons celery, finely chopped
4 tablespoons fennel, finely chopped

2 leeks, sliced
½ teaspoon tomato paste
salt to taste
freshly ground black pepper to taste
1 teaspoon cayenne, or to taste

Heat the olive oil in a large saucepan and sauté all the vegetables until they are well wilted. Then add the tomato paste and about 1 cup (120 ml.) water and simmer until all the vegetables are tender and most of the liquid has evaporated. Season to taste. *Serves 6.*

Variation:
The Ithacans prepare a collection of home grown and wild greens in a similar way but they sometimes stir in a cup of rice to the vegetables after sautéing them. The same formula is applied to many other vegetables, including leeks and celery.

Leeks with Rice

Prassórizo

🏛 CORFU

2 pounds (1 kg.) leeks, thoroughly washed
1 bunch of celery
cayenne and black pepper to taste
1/2 cup (120 ml.) olive oil

1 cup (250 g.) long grain rice
1 1/2 tablespoons tomato paste diluted
   in a little water
1/4 teaspoon sugar (optional)

Cut the leeks and celery into pieces measuring about 1 1/2 inch (4 cm.). Put them in a nonstick pan over a low heat so that they will exude their liquid. When they have reabsorbed it, add the cayenne and black pepper along with the olive oil and sauté gently for 5 minutes. Then add the rice, water to cover, and the diluted tomato paste (and sugar if desired). Simmer, covered, until the liquid has been absorbed and the rice is cooked. *Serves 4.*

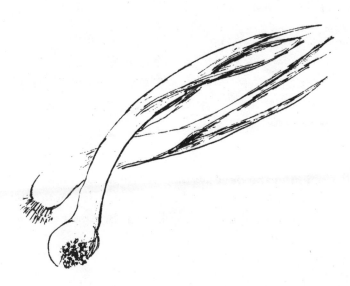

Potato Stew

Patátes yiachní

🏛 ZAKYNTHOS

We eat potatoes so often it is strange to remember the hostility this staple encountered when it was introduced to Europe. Greece has a Corfiot to thank for beguiling its population into accepting this tuber from the New World. Capodistrias, the first governor of Greece, had travelled widely in Europe, served as a diplomat for Russia, and spoken out for Greek interests at the Congress of Vienna. No doubt he had often sampled *potage Parmentier, pommes dauphines*, and a host of other delicious potato concoctions at state dinners. Moreover, he recognized it as a nutritious staple for a poor country. Once installed in the new capital at Nauplion, he tried to give potatoes away to the peasants. Being suspicious of handouts and conservative generally, they gave them a wide a berth. But Capodistrias knew his countrymen well and seems also to have been familiar with the similar tricks employed by Frederick the Great and Parmentier in Prussia and France. He had the vegetables surrounded by a fence and posted sentries to "guard" them round the clock. Before the week was out not a single potato remained.

For a Lefkadian dish, place some fried eggplant slices on top of the potatoes when they are nearly cooked.

1 medium onion, coarsely chopped
½ cup (120 ml.) olive oil
1 pound (½ kg.) ripe tomatoes, peeled, halved, and grated, or canned
2 pounds (1 kg.) potatoes, cut in large chunks

lemon juice to taste
salt to taste
freshly ground black pepper to taste

Sauté the onion in the olive oil until it wilts. Then add the tomatoes and stew them about 5 minutes before adding the potatoes. Simmer until tender and the liquid has thickened. Season with lemon juice, salt, and pepper. *Serves 4.*

Two Kinds of Baked Potatoes and Quince

Patátes, glykopatátes kai kydónia sto foúrno

🏛 CORFU

The Corfiots eat a lot of sweet potatoes. There are mounds of them in the open-air market, but their flesh is grayish rather than orange as in the U.S. This simple recipe is an unusual and delicious accompaniment to roast pork.

1 pound (¹/₂ kg.) white potatoes, quartered   *butter or margarine*
1 pound (¹/₂ kg.) sweet potatoes, quartered   *salt to taste*
¹/₂ pound (¹/₄ kg.) quinces, peeled, cored,   *freshly ground black pepper to taste*
*   and sliced (1 big one will do)*

Put all 3 vegetables in a roasting pan with some butter or margarine, salt, and pepper and bake in a moderate oven, 375° F. (190° C.), for 1 to 1¹/₂ hours, until tender and browned.

Soula's Spinach Pudding

Spanáki sto foúrno

🏛 CORFU

This could be called the "lazy cook's soufflé."

1 onion, chopped   *2 eggs, beaten*
2 pounds (1 kg.) spinach, well-washed   *¹/₂ cup (50 g.) kefalotýri or any*
*   and chopped (you can also use a*   *   hard cheese, grated*
*   packet of frozen spinach, thawed)*   *¹/₃ cup (75 g.) rice*
olive oil or ¹/₂ olive oil, ¹/₂ margarine   *¹/₃ cup (80 ml.) milk*

Sauté the onion and chopped spinach in olive oil or a mixture of half oil/half margarine until well wilted. Stir in the beaten eggs, cheese, rice, and milk. Mix well off heat and pour into a greased pyrex or baking pan, top with some more grated cheese, and cook in a moderate oven, 375°F. (190°C.), for about 40 minutes. *Serves 3 to 4.*

Stuffed Tomatoes

Domátes yemistés

🏛 CORFU

This recipe is a good example of the Corfiot love of herbs. The basil, mint, and parsley would have been growing in pots next to the kitchen door, the *máratho* (wild fennel), grabbed from the roadside (see page 61).

When this dish is made, other vegetables often accompany the tomatoes. Green bell peppers are frequently present, along with 1 or 2 eggplants or perhaps a medium-sized zucchini. This version is atypical in that it incorporates finely chopped peppers, cloves, cinnamon, and cayenne, which give the filling a much richer taste than the usual mainland dish.

The amounts given here will fill about 12 good-sized tomatoes and peppers. Don't worry about precise measurements, but don't overdo the cloves and cinnamon.

12 large round tomatoes	2 tablespoons fresh basil, finely chopped
salt to taste	2 tablespoons fresh mint or
sugar to taste	1 tablespoon dried
2 pounds (1 kg.) additional tomatoes, skinned, halved, seeded, and grated	2 tablespoons fennel leaves, finely chopped, optional
1 large onion or 2 medium, chopped	dash of ground cinnamon
2 small green bell peppers, finely chopped	pinch of ground cloves
2–3 cloves of garlic, finely chopped	cayenne pepper to taste
olive oil (at least ½ cup/120 ml.)	1 tablespoon tomato paste
3 tablespoons chopped parsley	8 tablespoons short grain rice

Preheat oven to 375° F. (190° C.). Slice the caps off the tomatoes and reserve. Scoop out the insides, taking care not to pierce the skins. Sprinkle the cavities with salt and a minute amount of sugar. Chop or grate the tomato mixture and place together with the rest of the grated tomatoes in a mixing bowl.

Sauté the chopped onions, peppers, and garlic in olive oil over medium heat, stirring so they don't start to scorch. When the vegetables are soft and about to brown, add the herbs and spices, stir thoroughly, and then add half the chopped tomatoes and the tomato paste. Cover for

a little while to make the tomatoes exude their liquid faster, and then add the rice. Cook, covered, over low heat until most the liquid has been absorbed.

Then remove from stove and fill each vegetable with the mixture. (Do not stuff too full or the tomatoes may split as the rice expands.) Put all the vegetables in a roasting pan and replace their caps. Pour the rest of the tomato puree mixed with additional olive oil, salt, pepper, and sugar over them. Bake for about 1 hour in the preheated oven and serve. These stuffed tomatoes are also wonderful cold (room temperature) the next day. *Serves 8 to 12.*

Variations:

If you want to make the Zakynthos version of this recipe, add ½ cup (90 g.) of hard, piquant cheese, cut in small pieces, to the vegetables just before you stuff them. The ideal cheese would be *ladotýri* from Zakynthos, but pecorino or *kefalotýri* are good substitutes. Half a cup of currants (75 g.) may also be added.

Some Zakynthians also put lots of chopped basil in the stuffing, which makes it quite green.

To adapt this recipe to include ground meat, just sauté ¼ pound (100 g.) of ground beef or lamb together with the onions, etc. until the meat loses its pinkness.

Many Greek cooks fill in the gaps between the vegetables with wedges of potato (especially if there are children to be fed), while in Zakynthos they may put in some okra as well.

Vegetable Bake
Tourloú or Ftohófago
🏛 CORFU

Tourloú (also called *Briám*) has often been referred to as the Greek cousin of ratatouille, and a poor relation at that if you encounter it in the usual taverna version, where it seems to consist mostly of potatoes with a few slender slices of zucchini thrown in. In Corfu, this dish is called *ftohófago*—a "dish for the poor"—but it tastes so delicious, it is really fit for kings or at least the new health-conscious White House.

The secret of success here lies in putting the vegetables in the baking dish in the proper order. Do not worry about exact amounts, but do make more than you think you need for one meal. It is even better the next day.

¹/₃ pound (150 g.) each of okra, string beans, zucchini (or more if you're using only one or two of these vegetables)
2 medium potatoes
2 green bell peppers
1 pound tomatoes
3 tablespoons olive oil or more

3 large onions
1 head garlic, cut in thin slices
1 bunch parsley, finely chopped
salt to taste
freshly ground black pepper to taste
sugar
3 tablespoons bread crumbs

Preheat oven to 375° F. (190° C.). Thinly slice all the vegetables except the okra and string beans—the latter should be cut in 2-inch (5 cm.) pieces, the former left whole.

Now take a 14 x 11 in. (34 x 27 cm.) roasting pan that is at least 4 inches (10 cm.) deep and coat the bottom with 1 tablespoon of olive oil.

1. Line the bottom with thinly sliced onions.
2. Place the okra, string beans and/or zucchini on top of them.
3. Add a layer of potatoes and green peppers.
4. Here you place another layer of finely sliced onions.
5. Cover with a layer of thinly sliced tomatoes.

Important: Between each layer, sprinkle a handful of parsley, salt and pepper to taste, and several slivers of garlic and drizzle the potato/pepper layer with the second tablespoon of oil and ¼ cup (60 ml.) water.

Top the last layer with a mixture of salt, pepper, and a little sugar to cut the acidity of the tomatoes. Then cover with bread crumbs and drizzle with more olive oil.

Cook in the preheated oven, until the vegetables are soft and the liquid has been absorbed (add a little more hot water if it looks dry prematurely). This should take about 1 ½ hours. Cover the pan with foil if you see that the tomatoes/crumbs are scorching. *Serves 6 to 8.*

Tip: If you've never liked okra because of its tendency to be slimy and furry at the same time, sprinkle it with salt and vinegar after trimming the tops, careful not to let the seeds escape, and set it in the sun for an hour or so. Then rinse. You'll find this treatment makes them most acceptable.

Vegetable Medley

Boutrídia

🏛 ZAKYNTHOS

Boutrídia is the Zakynthos version of *briám*; it means literally bits and pieces. As with the *ftohófago* above, you can use whatever vegetables happen to be available rather than sticking to the ones listed here. A country woman from the mountains gave this recipe to June.

¹/₂ pound (¹/₄ kg.) French or other green beans

1 pound (¹/₂ kg.) Swiss chard (silver beet, spinach beet, or beet greens)

1 medium eggplant, cut in chunks

3 medium potatoes, cut in chunks

¹/₂ pound (¹/₄ kg.) zucchini, sliced

¹/₂ pound (¹/₄ kg.) okra (see note page 191)

3 or more garlic cloves, crushed

¹/₂ cup (120 ml.) olive oil

2 pounds (1 kg.) ripe tomatoes, peeled, halved, and grated

salt to taste

freshly ground black pepper to taste

sugar to taste

Parboil the beans and chard separately for about 4 minutes, drain, and chop. Sauté the other vegetables (except for the tomatoes) in the olive oil. Put the chard, beans, and tomatoes in a baking dish with the other vegetables, season, and cook for about 1¹/₂ hours in a medium oven, 375° F. (190° C.). Peek at it from time to time and add a little hot water if it looks too dry. Serve with fresh bread and feta cheese. *Serves 6 to 8.*

Koula's Zucchini Fritters
Kolokithokeftédes
🏛 CORFU

Usually *keftédes*, from the Sanskrit *Kofta*, refers to meatballs. But the Greeks give the name to any mixture that has been formed into a ball and fried. Thus, there are *keftédes* made of potato, tomato, cheese, and even *taramá* paste. We have included two recipes for these fritters because both of them are so good.

Koula (Vassiliki Kapsokanadi) is a sparkling woman with a "magic spoon" who lives in Gastouri, one of Corfu's prettiest villages. She attributes the wonderful meals she produces to her constant attention to their cooking. "So many people just toss in all the ingredients and don't look at them again until they're done. They'll never get the same results as someone who stirs, pokes, bastes, and nudges the contents of the pan into goodness."

2 pounds (1 kg.) zucchini, grated	*½ pound (¼ kg.) kefalotýri or*
salt to taste	*Romano, grated*
1 bunch parsley, finely chopped	*freshly ground pepper*
1 bunch mint, finely chopped	*1–1½ cup dried bread crumbs*
2 medium onions, grated	*flour*
6–8 cloves garlic, finely chopped	*oil for frying*
2 eggs, beaten	

Put the grated zucchini in a colander, sprinkle with salt, and let stand for an hour so that they'll release their liquid. Meanwhile, chop the mint and parsley finely. Then squeeze the zucchini dry with your hands, a small amount at a time. Mix all the vegetables and herbs together along with the beaten eggs, cheese, and pepper. Then add the bread crumbs slowly, stirring until the mixture sticks together and is fairly solid. Make into patties, dust with flour, and fry in hot oil until lightly browned and crisp on the outside.

Soula's Zucchini Fritters

Kolokithokeftédes

🏛 CORFU

Soula adapted these fritters from her recipe for squash pie on page 164. Try both these and the preceding fritters; we're still trying to make up our minds which we prefer.

2 pounds (1 kg.) zucchini	*2 tablespoons parsley, finely chopped*
1 medium potato	*2 eggs, beaten*
1 large onion	*salt to taste*
1 cup (100 g.) hard cheese (kefalotýri,	*freshly ground black pepper to taste*
Romano, or dried myzíthra), grated	*2–3 tablespoons flour*
2 tablespoons mint, finely chopped,	*¹/₄ cup (60 ml.) milk*
or 1 tablespoon dried	*oil for frying*
2 tablespoons máratho (or fennel	
leaves), finely chopped	

Grate the zucchini, potato, and onion into a colander, sprinkle with salt (if desired), and leave to drain for about 30 minutes. Then take fistfuls of the grated vegetables and squeeze out their liquid. Add the cheese, herbs, eggs, and seasonings and mix well. Sprinkle the mixture with 2 to 3 tablespoons of flour, blending well with a wooden spoon. Then slowly add the milk until the consistency is like that of a thick, raw soufflé.

Heat about 1 inch of oil in a frying pan until almost smoking. Drop tablespoonfuls of the mixture into the hot oil as fast as you can and fry until golden-brown and crisp. Turn once or twice to crispen all over.

Drain on paper towels. Don't add too many spoonfuls to the oil at once or the temperature will drop and the fritters will be soggy. *Serves 6 to 8.*

BREADS
(Psomiá)

The Staff of Life for many generations in the Ionian was not wheat bread but corn bread. Corfu long ago even exported wheat so much was grown on the island. The Venetians changed all that; they permitted no crop that would conflict with their own interests. By the end of the seventeenth century the proliferation of the olive made any other cultivation unthinkable. Wheat flour became an imported luxury for all the islands. Though a recent novelty from the New World, corn was cheap and widely used to make bread in rural homes. In the twentieth century, when wheat bread was common once more, brown bread was peasant fare, while the townspeople ate bleached white loaves. Older Corfiots remember the delight on the farmers' children's faces when they were given a hunk of white bread. They thought it was cake. Nowadays, the preferences are reversed: sophisticates choose healthy, tasty brown bread, the descendants of those who knew nothing else prefer white bread.

Peasant Bread

Horiátiko psomí

🏛 ZAKYNTHOS

In Zakynthos, the peasant bread is made of whole wheat flour (*starénio*) the color of oatmeal. Unfortunately, modernity means that all the bran is sifted out of the flour. Traditionally, this bread should be made from a leavening of flour and an infusion of basil in hot water. The flour and basil used for the preparation of the leavening (or sourdough) should be blessed in the church at the celebration of the Day of the True Cross (*Imera tou Stavroú*) on September 14. This very moving ceremony, which June describes below, is gradually dying out and most of the Zakynthians, if they make bread at all, make it with baker's yeast.

"One year I went with my neighbor Kýria Katína to the local church in the village of Tragáki. Katína took with her a bunch of basil and a kilo of whole wheat flour wrapped in a white cloth. As we entered the church we were struck by the strong aroma of basil which pervaded it. This came from the dozens of baskets of basil laid at the foot of a large black wooden cross in front of the icon screen that separates the altar from the congregation. Everyone who came into the church placed their bunch of basil in the baskets; it was touching to see even little children entering the church clutching their bunches of basil. Basil is considered a sacred herb. According to legend, the place in the Holy Land where the True Cross was found was covered with it. Katína gave her bundle of flour to an acolyte to place on the altar, and I saw there was only one other bundle there—a proof, indeed, that this custom is dying out.

"There was also a shallow basket containing basil in which there were two metal crosses; one was placed upright amidst the basil together with three lighted candles. The basket of basil is called 'O Ipsoménon Vasilikós' (The Risen Basil). During the church service, the priest took the basket and held it high, then he placed it on a stand in front of the black cross and after walking around it with an incense burner, he placed the basket on the altar. Towards the end of the service every member of the congregation was given a bunch of basil from the baskets around the base of the cross. At its close, the priest also gave everyone a small sprig of the risen basil together with one or two pieces of sacramental bread (*Liturgía* or *Antídoro*). Katína was handed her flour from the altar.

"We then returned to Katína's simple kitchen, white and gleaming with aluminum pans, where I watched her prepare the leaven (*prozými*). She placed the risen basil in a bowl and poured boiling water over it. Then she let it reach

The basil ceremony

body temperature and strained it. She put the blessed flour into a large bowl, making a well in the center into which she poured the liquid from the steeped basil. Then she mixed it well to form a thickish dough. She shaped a cross with the stalks of the basil on top of the dough, covered it with a cloth and left it overnight. The next day Katína added some more flour and warm water, kneaded it well and left it again overnight. She repeated this process for a further two days before placing it in the refrigerator to be used as a leaven for her next batch of homemade bread. Katína told me that she could not give anyone her new leaven until forty days had passed, perhaps in memory of Christ's fasting in the wilderness."

Here is Kýria Katína's recipe for Peasant Bread.

11 pounds (5 kg.) whole wheat flour	*¹/₂ tablespoon baking soda*
(from durum wheat)	*¹/₂ cup salt*
3 cups of leaven (as described above)	*olive oil*
warm water	

Place two-thirds of the flour in a large bowl. Dissolve the leaven with warm water and then knead with the flour to make a softish dough, adding more warm water if necessary, and draw the dough to one side of the bowl. Sprinkle the rest of the flour on top and then wrap the bowl in woolen blankets and set aside for about 6 hours or overnight.

The next day (or 6 hours later), draw the sprinkled flour to the empty half of the bowl, mix with the soda and salt, and knead with warm water. Then knead the 2 doughs together for about 20 minutes. Lift the dough from the bowl and pour in about 4 tablespoons of olive oil. Then replace the dough and knead again. Divide the dough into 3 parts, after setting aside about 3 cups of dough for the next baking day.

Sprinkle some flour on a flat surface and shape the 3 parts into loaves of any shape you like, dipping your hands in warm water from time to time. Place the loaves in well-oiled baking tins, cover with clean cloths and leave to rise again for about one hour. Katína would bake her loaves in a wood-burning country oven. Failing that, pre-heat your oven to 400° F. (205 C.), bake for 20 minutes and then lower the heat to 300° F. (150° C.) and cook for another 40 minutes.

Corn Bread

Bobóta

🏛 ZAKYNTHOS

Although corn bread was a great staple in the Ionian Islands and in neighboring Epirus for centuries, it is not much appreciated in the rest of Greece because it is associated with the poverty and misery of the German and Italian Occupation during the Second World War. This recipe, however, is a festive spice bread with no resemblance to its more mundane namesake. The Zantiot bakers used to make this bread every morning. You could hear them shouting, *"Zestí i bobóta"* (hot bobota). Archduke Ludwig Salvator used to love it right from the oven spread with honey. He also says that housewives used to make another version that included herbs, pistachios, onions, and almonds, all finely chopped.

2 pounds (1 kg.) cornmeal

1 cup (240 ml.) orange juice

1 cup (240 ml.) olive oil

1 cup (100 g.) currants

1 cup (100 g.) walnuts, chopped

2 tablespoons orange peel, minced

1 teaspoon ground cinnamon

1 teaspoon ground cloves

2 teaspoons baking soda

1 tablespoon aniseed

Preheat oven to 375° F. (190° C.). Mix all the ingredients together, adding a little water if necessary, to form a stiffish dough. Place in 2 well-oiled bread baking tins and bake for about 1 hour. *Makes 2 loaves.*

Bread — Seven Times Kneaded

Eftázymo

🏛 ZAKYNTHOS

This is a fascinating way of making bread. It is baked on feast days, especially on Assumption Day (August 15th). The whole process is complicated by the fact that the rising agent is taken from the froth of soaked chick-peas. It is possible that this is one of the oldest methods of making bread, since chick-peas are one of the most ancient pulses and were cultivated in Homer's time under the name *erebinthus* (they are called *revíthia* in modern Greek). Chick-peas can still be found growing wild in the mountainous areas of Greece. June was told that when preparing this bread one should have a prayer book and a black-handled knife nearby!

In 1904, Archduke Ludwig Salvator wrote that in order for this bread to succeed one had to keep evil spirits away and prevent the devil from getting at it. He says the black-handled knife, a red blanket, and a holy book performed this function. The bread was made in each village in honor of its patron saint. The women who baked it would take it to church, where members of the congregation would leave a donation in exchange for a loaf. They would also distribute loaves among the houses, but this had to be carried out in complete silence for fear of attracting the attention of the evil spirits who would spoil the bread.

Here is an exact translation of the recipe given to June by a Zantiot peasant woman.

4 pounds (2 kg.) raw chick-peas	*1 bunch bay leaves*
1 pound (½ kg.) sugar	*1 handful fennel seeds*
1 cup (200 g.) mixed ground cinnamon,	*2 pounds (1 kg.) flour*
cloves and aniseed	

"Pound the chick-peas into small pieces. In the bottom of a large bowl, preferably earthenware or enamel, put three crosses of bay leaves and three of fennel seeds. Then cover all with bay leaves and then put a layer of crushed chick-peas 2 centimeters [⅔ inch] thick. Now put a layer of sugar and a layer of cinnamon, cloves, and aniseed and continue placing layers of chick-peas and spices until they reach the middle of the bowl. Before that have the spices soaking in boiling hot water. Then pour them into the bowl one finger's width above the mixture. Cover it with a woolen cloth and bury the bowl inside a bag of wheat or flour, so that it no air can reach it and the temperature stays a steady 50° to 60° C. [120° to 140° F.]. In 1 or 2 hours the mixture will begin to froth. Remove the froth with a spoon, mix it with 1 kilo flour and knead into a ball the size of an orange. Do this seven times until you have seven balls of dough. Then knead these again with more flour using very hot water to make a ball the size of a man's head. After this, you knead again with as much flour as you need and always with hot water at 50° to 60° C. When the dough is ready, make it into round loaves and put them on a special wooden board called a *pinakotí*. Then cover it with warm blankets at room temperature. When the loaves have risen, put them in the oven for one hour. Now you have the nice special bread called Eftázymo."

Traditional bread oven

Christmas Spice Breads

Christópsomo and Kouloúra

🏛 ZAKYNTHOS

These two sweet breads are eaten at Christmas. *Christópsomo* or Christmas bread has been compared to the Italian *panettone*, which it also resembles in appearance. The Zakynthians, however, are convinced that their recipe is incomparably more interesting. The *kouloúra* is made of the same dough but in the shape of a large ring; it is in here that the cook places the lucky coin to be found on Christmas eve.

When Private Wheeler was teaching school in Cephalonia, each of his "scholars brought a large loaf made of the best flour, covered with almonds and walnuts, in shape resembling a child in swathing bands and weighing from 6 to 14 pounds." The Ithacan *kouloúra* tastes of anise rather than nuts and spices. It is made of two rings of dough, braided with a cross and twisted and sculpted to represent the Virgin holding the baby Jesus in her arms. At Easter they cut the dough into concentric rings with spikes to look like an artichoke, with a red egg in the center and little dough birds perched on the rim.

2 pounds (1 kg.) flour

1 ounce (30 g.) fresh yeast or
    1 tablespoon dried yeast

1/2 cup (120 ml.) warm water

2 cups (480 ml.) warm red wine

1 cup (150 g.) currants

1 cup (150 g.) sultanas (raisins)

1 cup (150 g.) walnuts, roughly chopped

peel of 1 orange, finely chopped

peel of 1 tangerine, finely chopped

1/3 cup (50 g.) pignolia nuts (pine nuts)

2 cups (400 g.) sugar

1/4 teaspoon salt

1/2 cup (120 ml.) olive oil

2 teaspoons cinnamon

1/4 teaspoon powdered cloves

1/2 teaspoon anise, optional

FOR DECORATION

sesame seeds

whole walnuts

sugar

colored sprinkles, if available

Place the flour in a large bowl and make a well in the center. Put the yeast in a glass with the warm water and leave a few minutes. Stir the yeast and water until the yeast melts and then pour it into the flour together with the warm wine. Mix and knead well. Cover and leave to rise in a warm place for about 1 1/2 hours. Then mix in the rest of the ingredients.

Preheat oven to 425° F. (220° C.). Place on a floured surface and knead very well until smooth. Place the dough in a large oiled cake tin or for the *kouloúra*, in a tubular tin. Leave to rise again for about 30 minutes. Brush with olive oil and sprinkle with sesame seeds, sugar, and sprinkles. Decorate with walnuts. Bake for 15 minutes. Lower the heat to 375° F. (190° C.) and bake for a further 30 minutes.

Sweet Rusks

Paximádia

🏛 ZAKYNTHOS

This recipe is for a large quantity of rusks, but it can easily be halved. These rusks keep very well and are even more delicious when dunked in tea or coffee. They are not so much sweet as spicy.

3 pounds (1 1/2 kg.) flour
2 cups (480 ml.) olive oil
2 cups (400 g.) sugar
1 tablespoon ground cinnamon
1 tablespoon ground cloves
2 tablespoons aniseed
3 teaspoons baking powder

1 1/2 cups (225 g.) almonds or walnuts, blanched and chopped
2 cups (300 g.) currants
finely chopped peel of one orange
1–2 cups (240–480 ml.) wine (preferably red) or water
sesame seeds

Preheat oven to 375° F. (190° C.). Sift the flour into a large bowl. Heat the olive oil to body temperature and pour it over the flour. Knead well and then add the rest of the dry ingredients (except sesame seeds). After mixing them well, add enough wine or water to make a stiffish dough. Roll out the dough into "sausages" about 2 inches wide and slice off pieces 1 inch thick. Have the sesame seeds loose on a plate and roll each piece of dough in them. Then place the rusks on a well-oiled baking sheet and bake for about 1 hour. *Makes about 65 rusks.* (These can be stored for months in an airtight container.)

Olive Oil Rusks

Paximádia

🏛 KYTHERA

These are particularly satisfying to munch on when you're feeling peckish. The best ones are made in a small village in Kythera but the whole island adores them. The cinnamon taste should be very faint.

1½ ounce (40 g.) live yeast or	1 tablespoon salt
1½ packets	2 teaspoons powdered cinnamon
2 cups (480 ml.) warm water	(optional)
2 pounds (1 kg.) all purpose flour	1 cup (240 ml.) olive oil

Put the yeast in ½ cup (120 ml.) warm water. Sift the flour, salt, and cinnamon (if used) together and place in a bowl. Make a well in the center and pour the olive oil in it. Rub the oil into the flour with your fingers until it becomes like fine breadcrumbs. Mix the yeast and water together until the yeast melts. Pour it and the rest of the warm water over the flour mixture. Knead well together. You should have a stiffish dough. Place it in a bowl and cover lightly with plastic wrap and with a cloth. Leave it in a warm place to rise—about 1½ hours.

Place the dough on a floured surface and knead well until it is smooth. Form the dough into 2 loaves about 2½ inches (5 cm.) wide and cut the loaves into slices 1 inch (2½ cm.) thick. Place the slices on well-oiled baking sheets and cover. Leave undisturbed for about 30 minutes.

Bake in a preheated, very hot oven, 475° F. (250° C.), for about 14 minutes. Reduce the heat to 375° F. (190° C.) and bake for another 30 minutes. Remove the rusks from the oven and leave to cool. Then separate the rusks and place them on baking tins with plenty of room between them. Put them in a low oven, 300° F. (150° C.), for at least an hour. Switch the oven off and leave the rusks in it until they are completely cool. They should be very hard. *Makes 40 rusks.*

COFFEE AND DESSERTS
(Kafés kai Glyká)

We deciphered many of these recipes from tattered old notebooks, handed down from mother to daughter. Their compilers, who copied them down in spidery, old-fashioned writing, were far more interested in sweets than in main dishes, which did not need precise measurements. Exchanging recipes must have been a hobby in all the islands, for we found several names besides the owner's in every notebook, no matter its provenance. In earlier generations, elaborate ladies' tea parties were a popular and frequent social event, and no doubt each hostess made a considerable effort to outdo her friends in number and variety of cakes and sweets. Some of these recipes also reflect the cosmopolitan nature of Ionian society and its contact with English, French, and Italian cooking. The fact that some quantities were given in pounds and ounces, others in okes and drams, rather than the usual metric system, made them even trickier to get right.

Greek Coffee

A certain Professor Ansted visited the Ionian Islands in 1863, the year before they were to achieve independence, to report on conditions there. Here is what he had to say about his first drink of coffee in Lefkada. "The pure bean from Mocha, well and recently roasted, crushed between two stones; heated but never boiled in a most unpromising tin pot and finally poured out to be eaten rather than drank. . . . Nor is such a draught to be despised."

Archduke Ludwig Salvator, on the other hand, observed that in order to economize on coffee, the Zakynthians would grind it with roasted chick-peas and barley even in the coffee houses. Pure coffee had to be specifically requested and cost more. Many people also flavored their coffee with cinnamon or cloves. They also used to drink a good deal of sage tea (*faskómilo*), but he said the most common drink at the turn of the century was water boiled with honey.

Foreigners have often commented on the smallness of Greek coffee cups and the quantity of sludge at the bottom of them. Sometimes all one gets is a few sips of the drink, but with a glass of ice cold water a thimbleful can be made to last hours in an old-fashioned village *cafeneion*.

To make Greek coffee, you must have very finely ground coffee beans (they should be like a powder, even finer than for espresso). Allow 2 small coffee cups (demitasse size) of water per person and 1 heaping teaspoon of coffee. Put 1 teaspoon of sugar per person for sweet (*glykó*), ½ teaspoon or less for medium (*métrio*) and ¼ teaspoon to a pinch for slightly sweet (*me olígi*). Heat the water in a *bríki*, a small pot with a waist and a lip specially designed for coffee making, over a low gas flame. Before it boils, add the sugar. When the sugar has dissolved add the coffee. Stir constantly. To eliminate froth, bring to a simmer 3 times, taking it off the heat each time. Serve with a large glass of cold water.

English Pudding
Poudínga inglésiki
🏛 CORFU

This pudding used to be served in grand Corfiot houses. Obviously a legacy from the British Protectorate, it is rarely found nowadays. The woman who provided the recipe reminded us that its very simple ingredients tasted very different before the war, when eggs were fresh from the hen, the milk fresh from the dairy, and the apples had not been standardized to conform to European Union size and type regulations.

2 pounds (1 kg.) apples, half sour, half
    sweet, peeled, cored, and sliced
3 tablespoons sugar
3 tablespoons currants (optional)
3 thick rusks (or 6 thin ones), crushed
    (see page 64)

2 eggs
1 cup whole milk
grated rind of 2–3 lemons, juice of
    ½ lemon

Place the sliced apples in a baking dish and sprinkle with the sugar and the currants, if desired. Beat together the other ingredients and pour the mixture on top of them. Bake until firm in a moderate oven, 375° F. (190° C.), for 45 minutes. Serve with a *crème anglaise* or fresh cream. *Serves 6 to 8.*

Bread Pudding
Poudínga
🏛 CORFU

This pudding was considered an economical sweet and harks back to the British Protectorate. June's mother-in-law, who was half British, loved puddings. Her love was not shared by the younger members of her family, who made up a scornful song about her Roly Poly Pudding. They had to eat it all the same. This pudding met with greater favor.

1 pound (½ kg.) fresh brown bread crumbs
2 cups (480 ml.) milk
2 cups (400 g.) sugar
1 egg
2 cups (300 g.) currants
½ cup (75 g.) raisins

juice and peel of 1 bitter orange
    (or the juice of 1 lemon if bitter
    oranges are not available)
1 tablespoon or more melted butter
1 teaspoon cinnamon

You don't have to be too particular about quantities here. Just mix all the ingredients together, place in a buttered pan and bake in a preheated oven, 375° F. (190° C.), for about 1 hour. *Serves 6.*

Caramel Pudding

Poutínga

🏛 CEPHALONIA

This is another vestige of the British occupation, with perhaps some element of French influence, since it appears to be a combination of English trifle and *crème caramèle*.

CARAMEL

¹/₄ cup (60 ml.) water   *¹/₄ cup (50 g.) sugar*

First prepare the caramel. Boil the water and sugar together stirring constantly until the sugar melts and leave to boil without stirring until the caramel becomes a rich brown color. In the meantime, warm a round soufflé dish about 10 inches (24 cm.) in diameter, and when the caramel has cooled slightly, pour it into the dish, swirling it round and round to coat the sides and bottom.

¹/₄ pound (125 g.) lady fingers,   *4 eggs*
*   cut in small pieces*   *2 cups (480 ml.) milk, heated to body*
¹/₄ pound (125 g.) mixed glazed   *   temperature*
*   fruit, cubed*   *¹/₄ cup (50 g.) sugar*
¹/₂ cup (75 g.) almonds, blanched,   *¹/₂ teaspoon vanilla extract*
*   toasted, and coarsely chopped*   *grated rind of ¹/₂ lemon*

Preheat oven to 350° F. (175° C.). Place a third of the lady fingers in the bottom of the mold and sprinkle half the glazed fruit and half the almonds over them; repeat the process with the second third of the fingers and all the glazed fruit, adding the rest of the chopped almonds. Top with the remaining lady fingers.

Then beat the eggs, milk, sugar, vanilla, and lemon rind together and pour the mixture slowly over the pudding so that everything gets well soaked. Bake in a double-boiler for about 1 hour. Unmold before serving. *Serves 8.*

Kytheran Pudding

Poudínga apó Kýthera

🏛 KYTHERA

This is far richer than the original English semolina pudding.

5 cups (1.2 l.) milk	*1 teaspoon powdered cinnamon*
1 cup (150 g.) cream of wheat (semolina)	*1 cup (150 g.) raisins*
4 eggs, beaten	*1 cup (100 g.) blanched almonds,*
1 ¼ cups (320 g.) sugar	*finely chopped*

Preheat oven to 375° F. (190° C.). Heat the milk to body temperature and add the cream of wheat. Stir over a low heat until the mixture thickens. Remove from stove and leave to cool completely. Then stir in the beaten eggs and the rest of the ingredients. Pour into a buttered tin and bake for about 1 hour. *Serves 8.*

Fried Sweet Potatoes

Glykopatátes tiganités

🏛 CORFU

This dessert is most definitely home-grown. The Corfiot aristocracy are known for their genteel poverty. Though they may maintain some of the trappings of wealth—a gracious mansion (in need of repair) and a family retainer to serve at table—there were times when they did not have very much to eat. This little story illustrates the situation at one noble house just before World War II.

The lady of the house would preside over the long dinner table, ringing the bell for the maid, who wore a white apron and white gloves, when she was ready to be served. She spoke to her in Italian (or rather the Venetian dialect).

"Gintilitsa, *apporta el pesce*," she would command, and the maid would bring in a superb porcelain platter containing a few tiny fish. The maid would serve each person and retire. Then, when everyone had finished and the plates had been cleared, the hostess would again summon the maid, "Gintilitsa, *apporta el dorce*," and in she would come bearing another splendid platter with the humblest of desserts: slices of fried sweet potato sprinkled with a little cinnamon and sugar.

Elly's Orange Cream

Kréma portokalioú tis Ellis

🏛 ITHACA

We never met Elly, but she made this memorable pudding and gave the recipe to a friend who carefully added it to her collection.

Citrus trees were imported to the islands by the Venetians in the seventeenth century. Navel oranges, on the other hand, were introduced in the early twentieth century by an English businessman named Merlin, for whom they are named in Greek.

2 tablespoons flour	*peel of one lemon, grated*
1 cup (240 ml.) milk	*2 egg yolks, beaten*
1 cup (240 ml.) orange juice	*orange slices (optional)*
1 cup (200 g.) sugar	*whipped cream (optional)*
a few drops of lemon juice	

Mix the flour with a little of the milk and then slowly add the rest of the ingredients, except the orange slices, whipped cream, and egg yolks, stirring constantly. Pour into a saucepan and heat slowly, still stirring, until the liquid thickens. Then simmer for a few minutes longer. Let cool a little and then beat in the egg yolks. Pour into individual bowls and sprinkle with a little more sugar to prevent skin forming. Serve very cold. If you like, decorate with slices of orange and/or whipped cream. *Serves 6.*

Chocolate Cake

Toúrta sokoláta tis Haidós

🏛 ITHACA

This airy cake comes from another unknown friend of the Ithacan woman whose notebook we were lucky enough to find. Chocolate must have been rather a luxury for there are hardly any traditional recipes using it.

2 teaspoons baking powder
1 cup (150 g.) flour
1 cup (225 g.) butter
1 cup (200 g.) sugar
6 eggs, separated
1 cup (150 g.) cream of wheat (semolina)
4 tablespoons unsweetened cocoa or
  4 ounces (114 g.) baking
  chocolate (melted)

SYRUP

1 ½ cups (300 g.) sugar
3 cups (720 ml.) water
½ cup (120 ml.) brandy or coffee
  liqueur

Preheat oven to 375° F. (190° C.). Sift the baking powder and flour together. Beat the butter and sugar well together in a separate bowl and then add the egg yolks one by one, beating constantly. Stir in the flour mixture, semolina, and cocoa or melted chocolate and mix well. Beat the egg whites until stiff and fold into the mixture. Pour into a buttered, floured, round, shallow tin, 12 inches (30 cm.) in diameter, and bake for about 1 hour. Meanwhile, boil the ingredients for the syrup together for about 5 minutes and pour hot syrup over the cake, after it has cooled. Serve from the tin in squares or diamond-shaped portions. *Serves 10.*

Fasting Cake

Melachrinó (To Ftohó)

🏛 ZAKYNTHOS

Long and frequent fasting made the Greeks very resourceful in inventing ways of making things rich and tasty without the forbidden ingredients — butter and eggs. *Melachrinó* means "dark," *ftohó* means "poor," but there doesn't seem anything miserly or indigent about this list of ingredients.

2 pounds (1 kg.) durum wheat flour
¼ teaspoon salt
3–4 teaspoons baking powder
1 cup (240 ml.) olive oil
1 cup (240 ml.) orange juice
1½ cup (360 ml.) petimési
    (see page 63) or sweet wine
1 cup (200 g.) sugar

2 teaspoons ground cinnamon
2 teaspoons ground cloves
1 cup (150 g.) currants
1 cup (150 g.) walnuts, chopped
¼ cup (60 ml.) brandy
2 tablespoons orange peel, finely chopped
confectioners' sugar

Preheat oven to 375° F. (190° C.). Sift flour, salt, and baking powder together into a bowl, and then add all the other ingredients (except the confectioners' sugar). Mix well; if too stiff add a little water and if too runny add a bit of flour. Place in a well-oiled round baking tin, 12 inches (30 cm.) in diameter. Bake for about 1 to 1½ hours. When the cake has cooled, sprinkle with confectioners' sugar. Serve from the baking tin.

Sweet Rice Cake

Rovaní

🏛 ITHACA

Ravaní, as it is known in the rest of Greece, is a very popular cake saturated with honey. Some recipes call for at least two kilos of honey, but we have scaled this one down to an amount more acceptable to western tastes and pocketbooks. This Ithacan version is also unusual in that it calls for rice rather than the semolina used elsewhere.

1 ¹/₄ cup (375 g.) honey
²/₃ cup (175 g.) sugar
¹/₂ cup (120 ml.) olive oil
3 cups (720 ml.) water
1 cup (225 g.) short grain rice
1 ¹/₄ cup (40 g.) almonds, blanched,
   or ¹/₄ cup cloves (optional)

SYRUP
¹/₃ cup (100 g.) honey
¹/₃ cup (60 g.) sugar
¹/₃ cup (80 ml.) water

Place the honey, sugar, olive oil, and water in a saucepan and bring to a boil. Add the rice slowly, stirring constantly with a wooden spoon. Keep stirring over high heat for about 45 minutes. The rice should turn a golden color and absorb all the water.

Remove from the stove and set the pan in a basin of cold water so that the rice does not go on cooking and stick to the pan. Have ready an oiled round baking tin and spread the mixture evenly in it. Score the surface into triangles and place an almond or a clove in the middle of each triangle.

Bake in a hot oven, 450° F. (240° C.), until well-browned, about ¹/₂ hour.

Meanwhile, prepare the syrup by boiling the ingredients together for 5 minutes. Pour the syrup over the pie when done and then place in the oven again for the syrup to be absorbed. Let cool and serve. *Serves 8.*

Coconut Ravaní

Ravaní karýdas

🏛 CORFU

¹/₄ *pound (125 g.) butter*

1 cup (220 g.) sugar

3 eggs, separated

¹/₂ *pound (¹/₄ kg.) self-rising flour, sifted*

¹/₂ *cup (120 ml.) milk*

1 teaspoon vanilla extract

grated peel of ¹/₂ orange

¹/₄ *pound (125 g.) dessicated coconut,*
    plus some extra for decoration

whipped cream (optional)

SYRUP

1 cup (200 g.) sugar

1¹/₂ cups (360 ml.) water

3 cloves

2 sticks cinnamon

1 piece orange peel

1 tablespoon orange juice

Preheat oven to 375° F. (190° C.). Beat the butter and sugar together until fluffy and then add the egg yolks and beat again. Next add small amounts of the flour and milk alternately, mixing with a spoon, until they are both completely absorbed. Beat the egg whites until stiff and fold into the mixture. Finally, stir in the vanilla, orange peel, and coconut, until they are all evenly distributed. Spread the mixture in a baking tin (10 in./25 cm.) in diameter and bake for about 45 minutes.

While the cake is baking, prepare the syrup by heating all the ingredients together until the sugar melts, and cook for 5 to 10 minutes.

Let the *ravaní* cool before pouring the hot syrup over it. When the cake has absorbed the syrup, sprinkle it with some more grated coconut. Serve with whipped cream if desired. *Serves 10.*

Sponge Cake

Pandespáni

🏛 CORFU

In Zakynthos sponge cake and *soumáda* (a milky-colored drink made of almonds) are a traditional refreshment at weddings. But in Corfu friends used to send trays piled high with little iced sponge cakes after the birth of a baby. The arrival of a boy occasioned more cakes than a girl, but twins caused an avalanche. No one remembers how the tradition started, but some people think it may have been to make either the mother's milk or the baby's character sweet. You can vary the amounts in this recipe as you like so long as you keep the proportions the same.

4 eggs, separated
weight of the 4 eggs in sugar
1 tablespoon lemon juice
peel of ¹/₂ lemon
1 tablespoon water

weight of the 4 eggs in flour sifted
several times
confectioners' sugar (optional)

Beat the egg yolks until light and creamy and then gradually add the sugar, beating until the mixture becomes fluffy. Stir in the lemon juice, lemon peel, and water and then stir in the flour with a wooden spoon (not a mixer). Beat the egg whites until stiff and fold them into the batter. Pour into a shallow round buttered tin, 10 inches (25 cm.) in diameter, and bake for about 45 minutes. Cool before turning out. If desired, sift confectioner's sugar over the surface.

Mother of twins with cupcakes

Tangerine Cake

Keik mandarinioú

🏛 CORFU

2 cups (300 g.) flour
2 teaspoons baking powder
1 cup (200 g.) sugar
1 cup (225 g.) butter
3 eggs, beaten

½ cup (75 g.) raisins
peel and juice of 2 tangerines
⅓ cup (80 ml.) brandy or milk
confectioners' sugar

Preheat oven to 375° F. (190° C.). Sift the flour and baking powder together. Beat the sugar and butter together until fluffy. Add the beaten eggs and then add the raisins and the peel and juice of the tangerines. Mix in the flour and then the brandy. If necessary add more liquid (brandy or milk). The mixture should not be too thick, but of dropping consistency. Butter and flour a round tin, 10 inches (25 cm.) in diameter, pour in the batter and bake for 1 hour. When cool, turn the cake out of the tin and sieve confectioners' sugar on the surface.

Yogurt Cake

Yaourtópitta

🏛 CORFU

1 cup (225 g.) butter
2 cups (400 g.) sugar
1 cup (240 ml.) Greek strained
    yogurt (see page 66)
5 eggs, separated

1 teaspoon baking soda
peel of 1 lemon
3 cups (450 g.) flour, sifted
confectioners' sugar

Preheat oven to 375° F. (190° C.). Beat the butter and sugar together until light and fluffy and then add the yogurt, egg yolks, baking soda, and lemon peel. Mix well and then stir in the flour. In another bowl beat the egg whites until stiff and fold them into the mixture. Butter and flour a round pan, 10 inches (25 cm.) in diameter, pour in batter and bake for about 1 ½ hours. When cool, turn the cake out and sift confectioner's sugar over the surface.

Almond Tart
Pásta mílo
🏛 KYTHERA

This is a Kytheran specialty. It is reputed to have originally come from Smyrna. The only woman on the island who could make it refused to give the recipe to anyone, but just before she died she relented and whispered it to her daughter, who likewise refused to part with it during her lifetime. Again, however, when practically on her death bed, she revealed it to her godchild, who later gave it to anyone who asked for it. It used to be made only in the home but nowadays it is possible to buy it in local pastry shops.

PASTRY
½ cup (112 g.) butter
2 eggs, separated
2 cups (300 g.) flour

FILLING A
2 ¼ cups (250 g.) blanched almonds
1 cup (200 g.) sugar
½ cup (80 g.) semolina
1 egg white

FILLING B
2 cups (480 ml.) milk
½ cup (100 g.) sugar
½ cup (75 g.) cream of wheat (semolina)
2 whole eggs plus 1 yolk
1 teaspoon vanilla extract

You can use either this pastry recipe or the eggless one in the Basic Recipes on page 82.

First prepare the pastry by rubbing the butter into the flour and then adding the egg yolks and sugar. If necessary, add a little water to make a stiffish pastry dough. Cover with cellophane wrap and place in the refrigerator.

Preheat oven to 400° F. (205° C.). Mix the ingredients for filling A together and set aside. Prepare filling B. Heat the milk and sugar together and then throw in the cream of wheat. Stir well over a low heat until it thickens. Remove from heat and when it has cooled a little, stir in the beaten eggs and vanilla extract.

Line a round, shallow baking tin, 12 inches (30 cm.) in diameter, with the pastry, spread filling A over it. Pour filling B on top of filling A. Bake for 10 minutes. Lower the heat to 375° F. (190° C.) and cook for 35 minutes. When cool, decorate the top with glacé icing or Submarine Spoon Sweet (see page 233), or leave unadorned. *Serves 10 to 12.*

Pumpkin Pie

Kókkini kolokithópitta

🏛 ZAKYNTHOS

This pumpkin pie is a far cry from the American Thanksgiving Day favorite. Strudel-like, it is also very different from the savory version described on pages 164–165.

3 pounds (1 1/2 kg.) pumpkin, peeled
 and grated
1 cup (150 g.) currants
1 cup (150 g.) walnuts, chopped
1 cup (150 g.) almonds, blanched
 and chopped
1 cup (50 g.) rusk crumbs (see page 64)

1 1/2 teaspoons ground cinnamon
1/2 teaspoon ground cloves
4–5 tablespoons sugar
1/2 pound (1/4 kg.) fyllo pastry
 (about 1/2 packet)
4 tablespoons melted butter

Preheat oven to 375° F. (190° C.). Put the grated pumpkin in a saucepan and simmer until all its liquid evaporates. Now place the pumpkin and all the other ingredients (except the *fyllo* and melted butter) in a bowl and mix well. Place a sheet of *fyllo* pastry on the bottom of a medium-sized baking tin and brush it liberally with the melted butter; repeat the process with 2 more sheets and then spread the pumpkin mixture over them. Place 3 or 4 more sheets on top, one at a time, brushing each with the melted butter, as before. Trim off the surplus pastry and score the pie into squares. Bake for about 1 hour. *Serves 10.*

Variation:
As an alternative, you can also use this pumpkin mixture without the crust to make croquettes. Dust them with flour, fry them in piping hot oil, and then roll them in a mixture of sugar flavored with cinnamon.

Nut and Spice Rolls with Syrup

Rolá me sirópi

🏛 CORFU

These rolls look like Chinese spring rolls but their filling is similar to the English mincemeat used for Christmas pies.

½ cup (75 g.) sesame seeds

½ cup (75 g.) almonds, chopped

½ cup (75 g.) walnuts, chopped

½ cup (75 g.) hazelnuts, chopped

½ cup (75 g.) dried figs, finely chopped

½ cup (75 g.) dates or raisins, finely chopped

2 teaspoons powdered cinnamon

1 ½ tablespoons sugar

½ pounds (¼ kg.) fyllo pastry (see page 60)

melted butter

20 cloves

honey syrup (see basic recipe, page 83)

Preheat oven to 375° F. (190° C.). Roast the sesame seeds in a frying pan until light brown and then put them in mixing bowl. Add the nuts, figs, dates (or raisins), cinnamon, and sugar and mix well. Cut the *fyllo* sheets in quarters. Brush each piece with melted butter and place a heaping tablespoon of the nut mixture at one end. Fold the edges inward and roll up. Brush the roll with melted butter and place on a greased baking sheet. Repeat with the rest of the pastry. Set a clove in the center of each roll. Bake for about 20 minutes. Wait until the rolls have cooled before pouring the honey syrup over them. *Makes about 20 rolls.*

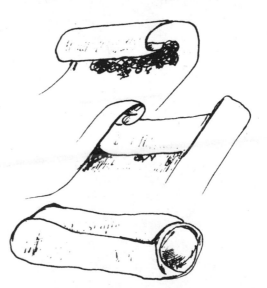

The Priest Wife's Walnut Pie

Karydópitta tis papadiá

🏛 CEPHALONIA

Could it be that all these measurements in "12s" were symbolic of the 12 Apostles? This is more like a rich cake than a pie. You can easily halve this recipe, if you like.

12 eggs, separated	½ teaspoon vanilla extract
12 tablespoons sugar	½ teaspoon powdered cinnamon
12 tablespoons chopped walnuts	½ teaspoon powdered cloves
12 tablespoons crushed rusks	2 teaspoons baking powder
grated peel of one lemon	2 tablespoons lemon juice
2 nutmegs, grated	

Preheat oven to 350° F. (175° C.). In a large bowl beat the egg yolks and sugar together until smooth and then gradually add the rest of the ingredients (except the egg whites, baking powder, and lemon juice), making sure they are well blended with each "dose." Next mix the baking powder and lemon juice together and add them to the bowl, stirring (preferably with a metal spoon). Finally, beat the egg whites until stiff and fold into the mixture. Pour into a large baking tin and bake for about ½ hour. *Serves 15.*

Fritters

Tiganítes or Loukoumádes

🏛 ALL ISLANDS

The Corfiots eat these luscious holeless doughnuts sprinkled with sugar and cinnamon, the Zakynthians with cinnamon and honey. They were a standard feature at name-day open house parties and guests often sent trays of them as presents. Vendors used to sell them door to door in Zakynthos town. (For more details on these see page 38.)

4 ounces (120 g.) yeast	*1 teaspoon salt*
1 cup (240 ml.) lukewarm water or	*vegetable oil for frying*
milk, plus about 1 cup water	*honey*
1 pound (½ kg.) flour	*cinnamon*

Dissolve the yeast in a basin with the cup of warm milk or water. Add 1½ cups of flour and put it to rise in a warm place until it doubles in volume. Then add the rest of the flour, the salt, and enough warm water (about 1 cup) to make a soft, fairly runny batter. Cover the basin with a dishcloth and let it stand in a warm place for at least 3 hours (up to 8 is fine) until it starts to form bubbles on top. The batter is now ready for frying.

Put about 3–4 inches (10 cm.) of vegetable oil in a deep saucepan and when it is steaming hot, drop a few small spoonfuls of batter at a time into the oil, and fry until golden. Dip the spoon into a cup of ice water each time before you dip it into the batter. This will prevent it from sticking to the spoon. Lift the fritters from the oil with a slotted spoon and drain on paper towels. Keep them in a warm oven while you cook the rest of the batter. Drizzle with honey and dust with cinnamon. Serve hot. The success of these fritters depends on having the oil hot enough and on keeping each spoonful about the size of a chestnut.

Allow about 5 *loukoumádes* per person. *This recipe will make about 40.*

New Year's Pastry Bows

Díples

🏛 ZAKYNTHOS

The name for these fritters literally means folded or pleated and refers to their
shape. Unlike the preceding *tiganítes* they do not need any yeast. These are
another very seasonal treat. Around Christmas and New Year's you see these
flattish bands of delicate pastry stacked in the windows of sweet shops all over
Greece. You also see lots of people of all age groups taking a break from their
shopping, trying to take a bite from a *dípla* wrapped in paper. It is almost impossible
to eat these without having their honey syrup drip all over you. Face, hands, and
clothes a mess, but how satisfying! They should be light as a feather.

3 eggs	*1 teaspoon baking powder*
3 ³/₄ cups (520 g.) fine semolina or	*¹/₂ teaspoon salt*
flour	*1 ¹/₂ cups (225 g.) walnuts, finely*
¹/₄ cup (60 ml.) milk	*chopped*
1 tablespoon olive oil	*1 tablespoon cinnamon*
¹/₂ cup (120 ml.) brandy	*honey syrup (see page 83)*

Beat the eggs well and add the semolina or flour slowly, stirring until
smooth. Then add the rest of the ingredients (except the walnuts,
cinnamon, and honey syrup). Knead well to form a stiffish dough.
Roll out the dough into a fairly thin sheet. Cut the dough into strips
about 4–5 inches (about 10 cm.) long and 2 inches (5 cm.) wide.
Then stick the two ends together and fold them into bows, triangles,
or pleats. Alternatively, just cut the dough into squares. Deep fry the
pieces in oil a few at a time until golden. Drain well on paper towels.
Arrange the *díples* on a large platter and sprinkle them with the
chopped nuts and cinnamon before pouring the honey syrup over
them. Serve cold. *Makes about 45 pieces.*

Fried Semolina

Fritoúres or Fitoúres

🏛 ZAKYNTHOS

These sweets are always made for *panagýria* (local church fairs) in Zakynthos. On these occasions stalls are set up where they are fried and sold on the spot. June thinks these are too stodgy for words, but her husband's aunt would die for them. Perhaps you have to have grown up in Zakynthos to truly appreciate them. Why not have a try?

9 cups (2 l.) water
1 pound (1/2 kg.) coarsely ground
   semolina
1/2 teaspoon salt

oil for frying
sugar
cinnamon

Bring the water to the boil and slowly add the semolina. Simmer until the mixture becomes fairly thick and then add the salt. Pour the mixture into a lightly oiled baking dish; it should be about 1 1/2 inches (4 cm.) thick. When it has cooled, cut it into squares and fry them in a little very hot oil. If you use too much oil, the mixture will crumble.

Eat immediately, sprinkled with sugar and cinnamon.

Fig Paste or Bread

Sykomaída or Sykópsomo

🏛 CORFU

This unusual delicacy appears in the fruit stalls on the island in autumn. It is apparently a very ancient confection; a few scholars even maintain that it was imported to Corfu from Pharaonic Egypt. The name is a composite of the words *sýko* (fig) and *mágis* (dough, paste, cake).

When Diana noticed this curious package among the greengrocer's offerings one November, he told her that it also contained orange peel, ouzo, fennel seeds, and black pepper. These various ingredients give it a pungent, "intriguing" taste. We will not give exact directions for making this but include this description from a book written in the nineteenth century as a matter of interest.

"When the figs ripen in late August and September, cut them cross-wise, open them and lay them in the sun to dry. When ready, chop them and put them in a bread-making trough and knead with fresh must [which would have been readily available at this time]. In the second kneading, add mastic [a liquor similar to ouzo] and chopped walnuts and almonds, plus some currants if desired. Make the paste into rounds about 6 to 8 inches in diameter like buns. Place on a baking sheet in a moderate oven. When all the moisture has evaporated, wrap in broad leaves—preferably chestnut or walnut—and tie up with string. Will keep until Easter."

ISLAND FRUITS
(Froúta nissiótika)

Wild Strawberries
Agries fraoúles

🏛 CORFU

Until a couple of decades ago, that is, before tourism became the island's number one industry, Corfu was famous for its wild strawberries. They were so fragrant that Olympic Airlines pilots refused to carry them on their flights back to Athens, saying that the smell made them dizzy. Now, because these *fraises des bois* take so much time to pick, they are a rarity and tremendously expensive, but if you happen to visit Corfu in May or June, do try to find some.

In Zakynthos, they are sold in little baskets lined with fern leaves and eaten with brandy and sugar.

Kumquats
Koúmkouats

🏛 CORFU

You might almost say that the kumquat has become the island's "national fruit," as it is so prevalent in all the souvenir and pastry shops. This diminutive member of the citrus family was reputedly imported to Corfu from the Far East in the middle of the nineteenth century. It was grafted onto more robust stock and since then has been put to a multitude of uses: glacéed, wrapped in chocolate, preserved, and made into a liqueur. This last, a virulent orange brew, is surprisingly good when added to a fruit salad or used as a marinade for tangerines mixed with strained yogurt and a little sugar.

Zakynthos Fruit

In 1682, George Wheler, Esq., wrote in his *Journey into Greece* that "here are the best Melons (I dare confidently say) in the World. . . . They are especially of two kinds, White or Yellow. . . . The Peaches here are extraordinary good and big, weighing from 10, to 15, to 20 Ounces. There are also Citrons, Oranges, and Lemons in abundance."

The reputation of Zakynthos melons has continued up to the present, though now other varieties have become more prolific.

COOKIES, CANDIES AND PRESERVES
(Biskótta Kai Glyká Tou Koutalioú)

Sesame and Honey Bars

Pastélli

🏛 ZAKYNTHOS

Here is a goody which is invariably served at *panigýria* and other celebrations. It is also packaged and sold in health food stores. A nutritious way to satisfy a craving for something sweet without consuming sugar, it would still probably horrify your dentist. Corfiots remember their excitement when as children they would watch the thick heady mixture being poured onto the marble, and their impatience at having to wait for it to cool before they could eat it. In Corfu, it has been called the "sweet of the young and the poor."

There is even a little jingle commemorating those days of hot *pastélli* and cold winters:

Vréhei, hionízei	It's raining, snowing
ta mármara potízei	watering the marble
i koukoútsa me to méli	the seed with the honey
ki i griá me to pastéli.	and the old lady with *pastélli*.

1 ¹/₄ pounds (600 g.) sesame seeds   *2 teaspoons orange peel, finely chopped*
1 pound (¹/₂ kg.) honey

Lightly brown the sesame seeds in a heavy frying pan. Heat the honey in a saucepan until boiling and then add the orange peel and the sesame seeds. Boil until a teaspoonful of the mixture poured into a glass of cold water does not disintegrate, but instead holds together. Then pour the mixture onto a marble slab or other smooth surface. Shape the mixture into a square about ¹/₂ inch thick and cut into bars 3 inches long and 1 ¹/₂ inches wide. They will keep for a long time (if your family doesn't gobble them down). Wrapping the individual bars in cellophane wrap will prevent them from sticking to each other. *Makes 30 bars.*

Sometimes *pastélli* is decorated with colored sprinkles or whole roasted almonds.

Walnut Balls

Troúffes apó karýdia

🏛 ZAKYNTHOS

This sweetmeat is surprisingly easy to make and wonderful to have around for the holiday season.

12 rusks (see page 64)   *brandy*
1 pound (½ kg.) shelled walnuts   *sugar*

Pound rusks and walnuts together until fine, or do the job with a food processor. Add brandy until you have a stiff dough. Then take small pieces of the dough and roll into small balls. Roll the balls in sugar and you have one of the quickest confections in your repertoire.

Almond Delights

Moustatsónia

🏛 CORFU

This almond cookie is only slightly more complicated than the one above and is another good staple with tea or coffee, or for midnight raids on the kitchen.

1 pound (½ kg.) almonds, blanched   *a dash of vanilla extract*
1 egg   *a dash of lemon juice*
1 cup (200 g.) sugar

Place the almonds in a food processor and grind until fairly well pulverized. Then add the egg, sugar, vanilla, and lemon juice and process until amalgamated. Remove the mixture and form into round flat cookies. Bake them in a medium oven, 300° F. (150° C.), until they are firm. They should *not* brown. They are apt to crumble so transfer them to a plate very carefully.

Spicy Almond Cookies

Rozédes

🏛 KYTHERA

*4 1/3 cups (640 g.) blanched and finely
    ground almonds*
1 3/4 cups (320 g.) sugar
1/2 cup (80 g.) cream of wheat (semolina)
2/3 cup (160 g.) honey

1/4 cup (60 ml.) water
1 teaspoon powdered cinnamon
1 teaspoon powdered cloves
confectioners' sugar (about 2 pounds/1 kg.)

Preheat oven to 375° F. (190° C.). Mix all ingredients except confectioner's sugar together until a thick paste forms. Wet your hands and take a tablespoonful of the mixture. Knead it well and roll into a small sausage, carefully forming it into an S shape (or any other shape if preferred). Repeat with the rest of the mixture. Place the cookies on a baking tin lined with aluminum foil brushed with melted butter. Bake for 20 minutes or until lightly browned. Leave to cool. Brush the cookies lightly with water and place them in a bowl of confectioner's sugar. Make sure they are all covered with sugar and leave them there overnight. *Makes about 40 irresistible cookies.*

Fasting Cookies

Kouloúria nistíssima

🏛 ITHACA

These would have been a Lenten staple in every island household in the old days.

¹/₂ cup (120 ml.) olive oil

1 cup (200 g.) sugar

³/₄ cup (180 ml.) orange juice

peel of ¹/₂ orange, finely chopped

¹/₂ tablespoon baking soda

1 teaspoon ground cinnamon

¹/₂ teaspoon ground cloves

¹/₄ cup (60 ml.) cognac or brandy

1 pound (¹/₂ kg.) flour

¹/₄ teaspoon salt

Preheat oven to 375° F. (190° C.). Mix all the ingredients together. The dough should be pliable. Roll out until the dough is ¼ inch (almost 1 cm.) thick and cut into shapes with a cookie cutter or even an empty jam jar. Bake on oiled cookie sheets until light brown — about 20 minutes. *Makes 45 cookies.*

Spoonsweets
Glyká tou koutalioú

The Greeks make an infinite variety of what they call spoonsweets, what we would call preserves. It is a delightful habit, though fast dying out among the younger generation, after a siesta on a hot summer's afternoon to savor a spoonful of preserve accompanied by a glass of iced cold water. The intense sweetness wakes you out of your lethargy and seems to propel the energy flowing back through your body. These preserves were not used to spread on bread but were (and still often are) offered in a gesture of hospitality to visitors. They were usually followed by a glass of liqueur.

June's father, whose ancient Greek was unintelligible and whose modern Greek was nonexistent, nevertheless had caught on that when the liqueurs appeared the visit was nearing its end. Delightful crystal containers exist for these preserves, usually with silver spoons hanging around them; their design originated in Constantinople.

There used to be an elaborate protocol associated with the serving of these sweets, as an authority on Cephalonian society informed us. First-class visitors were treated to diamond-shaped pieces of quince paste or a spoonful of preserves, accompanied by coffee, liqueurs, and a glass of cold water. The quince paste and liqueurs were omitted if the visitor merited only second-class treatment, while a person of no consequence received only coffee and water. What is all the more remarkable is the value set on them by the very poor. Although some rural houses had very little furniture, they invariably had a chest for storing foods, and within that chest was a locked compartment where the spoonsweets were hoarded, for they were rarely if ever wasted on mere family.

Greek housewives preserve almost any fruit, the most common candiates being strawberry, quince, apple, peach, apricot, morello cherry, baby fig, orange peel, seedless grapes, pear, and watermelon rind. More unusual preserves are made from kumquats, pistachio nuts, pumpkin, bergamot, fresh walnuts, and baby eggplant.

In the modern era they are a delicious topping for thick Greek yogurt. The seedless grape and quince preserves are especially suitable.

There is also a strange spoonsweet called *ypovrichion* (submarine) which resembles sugar fondant. It can either be white and flavored with vanilla or mastic, or pink and tasting of rose petals. Children love to suck on a tablespoonful of the stuff, dunking it into a glass of iced cold water between each lick.

Pear Preserve
Achladáki glykó
🏛 ALL ISLANDS

4 pounds (2 kg.) small pears	*¼ pounds (125 g.) blanched almonds*
5 cups (1.2 l.) water	*4 pounds (2 kg.) sugar*
5 lemons	*3 teaspoons vanilla extract*

Wash and peel the pears. Keeping them whole, remove the cores, and place the pears in a bowl of water with the juice of 2 lemons. When you are ready to cook them, remove the pears and put an almond or two inside each one. Boil 2 cups of sugar with the water and 2 tablespoons of lemon juice for 5 minutes, stirring well. Put the pears in the syrup and boil for 10 minutes. Add the rest of the sugar and boil again for 10 minutes stirring well. Leave for 24 hours and then cook them again until the syrup sets. Add the juice of 2 lemons and the vanilla. Pour into sterilized jars. If you have difficulty in coring the pears, cut them into halves or quarters to remove cores, and just mix the almonds with the preserve.

Seedless Grape Preserve
Sultanína glykó
🏛 ALL ISLANDS

4 pounds (2 kg.) seedless grapes
2 pounds (1 kg.) sugar
½ cup fresh orange juice

1–2 sprigs rose geranium
(if available)
2 teaspoons vanilla extract

Remove the grapes from the stalks and wash well. Drain and place in a saucepan in layers with the sugar sprinkled in between. Pour the orange juice over them. Leave in the refrigerator for at least 12 hours. Bring the grapes to the boil, stirring constantly until the sugar dissolves. Boil for 10 minutes. Leave for 24 hours. Add the rose geranium (if used), and boil for about ½ an hour until the syrup sets. Stir in the vanilla extract. Pour into sterilized jars.

Strawberry Preserve
Fraoúla glykó
🏛 CORFU

3 pounds (1½ kg.) underripe strawberries
juice of three lemons
3 pounds (1½ kg.) sugar

2 cups (480 ml.) water
2 teaspoons vanilla extract (optional)

Hull and wash the strawberries and spread them on a cloth to dry. When dry, place the berries in a bowl with the lemon juice and mix lightly. Put the sugar and water in a saucepan and boil, stirring until the sugar dissolves and the syrup thickens. Then add the strawberries and bring back to the boil. Remove from the heat and leave to cool. Lift out the strawberries and place them carefully on a platter. Boil the syrup again until it begins to set. Remove at once from the stove and add the strawberries (and vanilla, if used). Leave to cool before pouring into jars. Do not cover until cold.

The following two sweets are candies rather than preserves. They also would have been offered to friends or acquaintances who happened to drop in.

Peach Preserve

Rodákino glykó

🏛 CORFU

3 pounds (1 ½ kg.) not-too-ripe peaches   juice of 2 lemons
1 cup (240 ml.) water   3 pounds (1 ½ kg.) sugar

Peel the peaches, cut into quarters, and immediately put them in a bowl of cold water acidulated with the juice of 1 lemon so that they do not discolor. Strain the peaches and place them in a saucepan with the sugar and water. Bring to the boil, stirring until the sugar dissolves. Continue to boil until the syrup sets. Add the juice of 1 lemon and leave to cool somewhat before pouring them into jars. If any of the pieces of peach begin to break remove them and add to the syrup at the end of cooking.

Almond and Tangerine Sweet

Amýgdalo kai mandaríni glykó

🏛 CORFU

6 tangerines   1 ¼ pounds (625 g.) sugar
water   juice of 3 to 5 tangerines
1 pound (½ kg.) almonds, blanched

Boil the 6 tangerines in enough water to cover for about 5 minutes to remove their bitterness. Peel and place the tangerine skins with the almonds in a food processor and puree until smooth. Scrape into a bowl and add the sugar and the tangerine juice. Mix well. Put the mixture in a saucepan and boil until the liquid evaporates. When cool, form into balls the size of a walnut. Dip them in sugar and leave to dry.

Quince Delight
Loukoúmia kydonioú
🏛 CORFU

Loukoúmia is the word for what westerners usually call Turkish delight. Sometimes overly plump little boys are also referred to as "loukoúmia" in Greece.

6 quinces

sugar, 1 ¼ pounds (625 kg.) for each pound (1 ½ kg.) of cleaned quince

rose water, to taste

4 ounces almonds, chopped, optional

confectioners' sugar

Boil whole quinces until soft. When cool, peel and core them and cut into pieces before sieving or pureeing them in a food processor. Place the quinces and the sugar together in a saucepan and boil until you have a thick puree. Add a few drops of rose water and some roasted, chopped almonds, if liked. Pour into a square or oblong tin and leave overnight. Cut in bite-sized squares and dip in confectioners' sugar. Leave for a second night and then dip them a second time in the sugar.

Quince Sauce
Moustárda
🏛 CORFU & ZAKYNTHOS

There is an Italian relish with this name that is more like a pickle, but it is very different from this sauce, which is eaten over the Christmas holidays as an accompaniment to roast pork, lamb, or game. Without the mustard, it resembles apple sauce and is sometimes spread on bread for a quick snack. The Corfiots also make a kind of apple chutney, which Laurence Durrell listed as being among the few vestiges of English rule.

Cut unpeeled quinces into cubes and boil them in must or sweet wine with ground cloves to taste, until thick. Place in a bowl and mash well, adding powdered mustard (Colman's English) to taste. This sauce will keep for some time if refrigerated.

Nougat
Mandoláto zakynthinó
🏛 ZAKYNTHOS

Definitely the best nougat in the world! Or so the Zakynthiots claim. You see these white nutty slabs piled in mounds or wrapped in boxes in all the tourist shops on the island. It is made on all the Ionian Islands (except Kythera, Paxos, and Ithaca), but the Zakynthos version is the chewiest and has been the most sought after since Venetian times. It was considered an indispensable addition to the table over the Christmas holidays and during Carnival, and at the turn of the century the island sold some twenty thousand pounds of the stuff each year.

When Archduke Ludwig Salvator visited Zakynthos in 1904, he noted the following method of making *mandoláto*, which is enough to deter even the most enthusiastic cook. It came from the best confectioner's in Zakynthos, which was founded in 1841. "First, you must heat local honey in a copper cauldron over a low flame and stir it for about 1 hour with a special wooden paddle. The honey must never be hot enough to burn your fingers. As soon as the honey develops threads when removed from the fire, add well beaten egg whites and go on stirring for another 4 hours. You'll know it's ready if a bit of it starts to dissolve when dipped into cold water. Then mix in some roasted almonds and cool on a marble slab. Pistachios can be added instead of almonds if the nougat is intended for the elderly," and of course it can be made in less time, in which case it will be sold more cheaply. (The usual dose for a pound of honey was 3 egg whites and half a pound of almonds.)

Our recipe is less arduous and has more ingredients than the Archduke's.

1 pound (¹/₂ kg.) sugar
1 cup (240 ml.) water
2 drops lemon juice
1 pound (¹/₂ kg.) honey
4 egg whites
1¹/₄ pounds (700 g.) almonds, blanched,
*   roasted, and roughly chopped*

1 cup (150 g.) pistachio nuts, whole
*   and roasted*
1 teaspoon coriander seeds, ground
peel of one orange, minced
6 sheets of fyllo *pastry*

Preheat oven to 375° F. (190° C.). Boil the sugar with half the water and the lemon juice until it becomes a thick syrup, taking care not to let it color. Boil the honey with the rest of the water for 5 minutes and mix the 2 liquids together.

Beat the egg whites until stiff and then fold into the liquid.

Place the saucepan with the mixture over low heat and stir with a wooden spoon. As soon as it is hot, add the almonds, pistachios, coriander, and orange peel, stirring gently but constantly until the mixture sticks together. Remove from heat and cool.

When the mixture has cooled off, lay 3 sheets of *fyllo* pastry on top of each other on a flat surface and spread the mixture over them. Put the remaining 3 sheets on top and press with a chopping board to bind everything together. Then cut the nougat into squares and place them in a baking tin. Cook for about 15 minutes.

ACKNOWLEDGMENTS

So many people have contributed to the making of this book that we would like to take one short page to thank them. Some of them contributed recipes and anecdotes, others helped with the text, and still others offered much needed encouragement. Listing their names here is a small token of our immense gratitude.

First, on the islands, our research was generously assisted by Helen Cosmetatos, Philenni Damaskinou, Alekos Damaskinos, Cali Doxiadis, Victoria Drew, Aleka Frederikou, Erofili Gigantes, Lady Marjorie Holmes, Vassiliki Kapsokavadi, Boula Kondi, Maria Kostara, Christopher Lavranos, Marily Macvicar, Dionysios Marinos, Panayotis Marinos, Georgia Marinos, Anna Merlin, Andreas Papadatos of the Corfu Reading Society, Andreas Roussopoulos, and Anastasia Spyrou.

In Athens, Susie and Zikos Tassios, John Chapple, Aliki Chapple, Petros Ladas, and Sue Camarados all provided invaluable advice, and the Gennadios Library and the Library of the British School at Athens were treasure troves of fascinating material.

No words are adequate to thank Themistocles Marinos for his indefatigable support, knowledge of island lore, and multiple rereadings of the text, and Judy Lawrence, not only for her delightful drawings but also for her wit and wisdom pertaining to literary and culinary aspects of the text.

Finally, we extend our appreciation to Harilaos Louis, our families and friends, and June's bridge group for their patience, understanding, and enthusiastic tasting of the recipes from Prospero's and our kitchens.

BIBLIOGRAPHY

Ansted, D.T., *The Ionian Islands in the year 1863* (W. H. Allen & Co., London, 1863).

Beeton, Isabella, *Beeton's Book of Household Management* (Farrar, Straus & Giroux, New York, 1969).

Bellaire, J.P., *Compagne à Corfou* (Paris, 1805).

Carlisle, Earl of, *Diary in Greek and Turkish Waters* (Longman, Brown, Green and Longmans, London, 1855).

Chatto, James & W.L. Martin, *A Kitchen in Corfu* (Weidenfeld & Nicolson, London, 1987).

Davy, John, *Notes and Observations on the Ionian Islands and Malta* (Smith & Elder, London, 1842).

Doikas, Yianis, *Paxos* (1985).

Durrell, Gerald, *My Family and Other Animals* (Penguin, Middlesex, 1965).

Durrell, Lawrence, *Prospero's Cell* (Faber & Faber, London, 1962).

Finlay, George, *The History of Greece under Ottoman and Venetian Domination* (Wm. Blackwood & Sons, Edinburgh & London, 1856).

Homer, *Odyssey*, trans. Robert Fitzgerald (Vintage, New York, 1961).

Homer, *Iliad*, trans. Richard Lattimore (University of Chicago Press, Chicago, 1961).

Hytiris, Ger. *Ta Laografiká tis Kerkýras* (Corfu, 1991).

Jervis, Henry Jervis-White, *History of the Island of Corfu and of the Republic of the Ionian Islands* (Colburn & Co., London, 1852).

Kathimerini Sunday Magazine, "O politismós tis Elaiás" (Athens, 16 Jan. 1994).

Kathimerini Sunday Magazine, "Xehasména Nisiá tis Elládas" (Athens, 23 Oct. 1994).

Kendrick, Tertius T.C., *The Ionian Islands* (James Haldane, London, 1822).

Kirkwall, Viscount, *Four Years in the Ionian Islands* (2 vols) (Chapman & Hall, London, 1864).

Kochilas, Diane, *The Food and Wine of Greece* (St. Martin's Press, New York, 1990).

"The Other Side of Kerkyra's Culinary Track," in *Athens News* (4 Nov. 1994).

Kythera, Paradosiakés Syntaghés, ed. Syntrofiá ton Kytheríon Kyrión tou Trifylleíou Idrýmatos (Kythera, 1987).

Lambert-Gocs, Miles, *The Wines of Greece* (Faber & Faber, London, 1990).

Lampedusa, Giuseppe Tomaso di, *The Leopard*, trans. Archibald Colquhoun (Pantheon, New York, 1960).

Lear, Edward, *The Corfu Years*, ed. Philip Sherrard (Denise Harvey, Athens, 1988).

Manessis, Nico, *Greek Wine Guide* (Olive Press, Athens, 1994).

Miller, William, *The Latins in the Levant* (Speculum Historiale, Cambridge, 1964).

Montagne, Prosper, *Larousse Gastronomique* (Crown Publishers, New York, 1961).

Morris, James, *Venice* (Faber & Faber, London, 1960).

Murray's *Handbook for Travellers in Greece* (London, 1872).

Napier, Charles James, *The Colonies* (Thos. & Wm. Boone, London, 1833).

Pratt, Michael, *Britain's Greek Empire* (Rex Collings, London, 1978).

Salvator, Archduke Ludwig, *Zante* (Prague, 1904).

Simeti, Mary Taylor, *Pomp and Sustenance* (Henry Holt & Co., New York, 1991).

Stavroulakis, Nicholas, *Cookbook of the Jews of Greece* (Lycabettus Press, Athens, 1986).

Theodosis, Dinos, "I Voúta stou Ayiánnou to kandoúni," in *Próodos tis Zakýnthou* (8 April 1994).

Theotokis, Emmanuel, *Détails sur Corfou* (1826).

Tsitsas, A.H., *Kérkyra, Nostalgikés Anadromés* (Society for Corfiot Studies, Corfu, 1992).

Tuckerman, Charles K., *Greeks of Today* (G.P. Putnam & Sons, New York, 1873).

de Vaudoncourt, Guillaume, *Memoir on the Ionian Islands* (Baldwin, Cradock & Joy, London, 1816).

Wheeler, Private, *The Letters of Private Wheeler*, ed. Capt. B.H. Liddell Hart (Michael Joseph, London, 1951).

Wheler, George, *A Journey into Greece, in company with Dr. Spon of Lyons* (London, 1682).

Young, Martin, *Corfu and the other Ionian Islands* (Jonathan Cape, London, 1981).

INDEX

achinosaláta, 91

achladáki glykó, 233

agries fraoúles, 225

allspice, 65

almond and tangerine sweet,
    235

almond cookies, spicy, 230

almond delights, 229

almond tart, 217

amýgdalo kai mandaríni glykó, 235

angináres kokkinistés, 178

angináres psités sta kárvouna, 92

angináres tiganités, 92–93

angináres yemistés, 177

*arní sto foúrno me rísi kai
    yiaoúrti*, 149

artichokes:
    fried, 92–93
    grilled, 92
    stewed, 178
    stuffed, 177

avgá me domáta sáltsa, 114

avgá skordostoúmbi, 113

avgá strapadsáda, 112–113

avgolémono, 38, 84, 103

ayáda, 96

bakaliáro bourdétto, 120

bakaliáro me prássa, 121

basil, 61

bay leaves, 61

bean soup, multi-, 106–107

bean soup, Zakynthos, 105

béchamel sauce, 83

beef:
    cottage pie, 156
    meat and rice croquettes,
        155
    meat loaf, 153
    meat pie, Cephalonian,
        170–171
    meat pie, Corfiot, 174
    meat pie, Lefkadian, 173
    meatballs, 152
    moussaka, Soula's, 154–155
    pot roast with parsley, 148
    ragout with macaroni, 146
    with garlic and parsley, 144
    Venetian pasticcio, 168–169
    Zakyntian ragout with
        macaroni, 147
    Zante ragout, 145

bekátsa salmí, 141

bianco, 122

bobóta, 199

boubourélla, 106–107

bourdétto me kéfalo, 126
bourdétto Paxón, 123
bourdetto with grey mullet,
    126
boutrídia, 192
bread, 195
    cheese, 112
    Christmas spice, 41,
        202–203
    corn, 199
    fig, 224
    olive oil rusks, 204
    peasant, 196–198
    seven times kneaded,
        200–201
    sweet rusks, 203
bread pudding, 207
broccoli:
    Zakynthos style, 181
brokolínes, 181

cabbage and arugula salad, 108
cake:
    chocolate, 211
    coconut ravani, 214
    fasting, 212
    fig, 224
    sponge, 215
    sweet rice, 213
    tangerine, 216
    yogurt, 216
    see also pastry and sweets,
        pies, *and* tarts
candy. *See* pastry and sweets
caramel pudding, 208

cayenne, 65
celery, 61
cheese and garlic dip, 97
cheese, 59–60, 111
    pie without trousers, 112
chick-pea soup, 104
chicken, 131;
    from the village of Agala,
        135
    casserole roasted, 136
    roasted, Soula's, 132
    stewed, 133
    stuffed roasted, 134,
        136–137
    Venetian pasticcio, 168–169
    see also poultry
chocolate cake, 211
Christmas spice bread, 41,
    202–203
Christópsomo, 41, 202–203
cinnamon, 65
cockerel, stewed, 133
coconut ravani, 214
cod:
    cod-roe dip, 88
    see also salt cod
coffee, 205
    Greek, 206
cookies:
    almond delights, 229
    fasting, 231
    spicy almond, 230
corn bread, 199
Cornish game hens:
    pilaff, 140

Cornish game hens (*cont.*):
  salmi, 141
  stuffed, 139
  with broad beans, 142
cottage pie, glorified, 156
croquettes, meat and rice, 155
cuttlefish with celery, 128

desserts, 205. *See also* cake,
    cookies, fritters, pastry
    and sweets, pies, spoon-
    sweets, *and* tarts
dill, 61
dip:
  cheese and garlic, 97
  cod-roe, 88
  eggplant, 93
  garlic, 96
  herring-roe, 89
  yellow split pea puree, 99
díples, 222
domátes iliópiastes, 94
domátes yemistés, 188–189
domatósoupa yia Sarakostí, 101

eftázymo, 200–201
egg-lemon sauce, 84
egg-lemon soup, 38, 46, 84
  with turkey, 103
eggplant:
  dip, 93
  salad, 94
  smothered in garlic, 180
  stuffed with parsley and
    cheese, Soula's, 179

eggs, 111
  piquant poached, 114
  scrambled, with tomatoes,
    112–113
  smothered in garlic, 113
Elly's orange cream, 210
English pudding, 206–207

fakés kai patatosaláta, 110
fasoláda, 105
fasting cake, 212
fasting cookies, 231
fáva, 99
fennel, 61
  and orange salad, 109
féta kai skórdo mezé, 97
fish, 117
  baked with wine, 125
  cod-roe dip, 88
  cuttlefish with celery, 128
  herring roe dip, 89
  Kythera style, 124
  marinated, 118
  seafood casserole, 128–129
  see also fish soups and stews,
    mussels, octopus, sea
    urchins, *and* squid
fig bread, 224
fig paste, 224
fish soups and stews, 102, 119
  bourdetto with grey mullet,
    126
  fish stew, 122
  fish stew from Paxos, 123
  salt cod stew, 120

fish soups and stews (*cont.*):
    salt cod stew with leeks, 121
fitoúres, 223
fraoúla glykó, 234
fritoúres, 223
fritters:
    Koula's zucchini, 193
    semolina, 223
    Soula's zucchini, 194
    sweet, 221
ftohófago, 190–191
fyllo, 60

garlic, 60
    eggs smothered in, 113
    fried fresh, 98
garlic dip, 96
    with cheese, 97
garlic sauce, 56, 96
glykopatátes tiganités, 209
grape preserve, seedless, 234
greens, 55, 182
    Ithacan, 184
    sauteed, 182–183
    stewed, 184

ham, spiced, 151
hare:
    Cephalonian ragout, 158
    ragout, 157, 160
    see also rabbit
herbs, 60–66
herring-roe dip, 89
hirinó yemisto, 150–151
hiroméri, 151

honey, 62
honey syrup, 83
horiátiko kotópoulo apó ton Agalá,
    135
horiátiko psomí, 196–198
hórta, 55, 56, 182
hortópitta, 166

kalamarákia me rísi, 127
karyðópitta tis papaðiá, 220
kefallonitikí kreatópitta, 170–171
keik mandarinioú, 216
kókkini kolokithópitta, 218
kolokithokeftéðes, 193, 194
kolokithokorfáðes, 100
kolokithópitta, 164–165
kotópoulo in úmiðo, 136
kotópoulo psitó, 132
kotópoulo psitó yemistó, 134,
    136–137
Koula's green pepper and
    potato salad, 110
Koula's zucchini fritters, 913
kouloúra, 202–203
kouloúria nistíssima, 231
koúmkouats, 225
kounéli me skórðo, 159
kounéli sto foúrno me patátes, 161
krabí kai róka saláta, 108
kreatópitta Kerkýras, 174
kreatópitta tis Ithákis, 172
kreatópitta tis Lefkáðas, 173
kréma portokalioú tis Ellis, 210
krokéttes, 155
ktapóði psitó sto foúrno, 90–91

ktapódi toursí, 90
ktapódi yachní, 126–127
kumquats, 225
kythiriótiko psári, 124

láchano bourdétto, 184
lagotó, 158
lamb, 47, 53
    baked with rice and yogurt,
        149
    Cephalonian ragout, 158
    innards with egg-lemon
        sauce, 162
    Ithaca meat pie, 172
    meat pie, 170–171
    Soula's moussaka, 154–155
    Venetian pasticcio, 168–169
leek pie, 164
leeks with rice, 185
lentil and potato salad, 110
lentil soup, 106
loukoumádes, 221
loukoúmia kydonioú, 236

macaroni with false ragout
        sauce, 115
makarónia me pséftiki sáltsa, 115
mandoláto Zakynthinó, 237–238
manitária marináta, 98–99
marjoram, 62
mayonnaise, 83
mayonéza, 83
Mavrodaphne wine, 63, 78–79
meat, 143; *see also* beef, ham, hare,
        lamb, pork, rabbit, *and* veal

meat loaf, 153
meat pie, 163
    Cephalonian, 170–171
    Corfiot, 174
    Ithacan, 172
    Lefkadian, 173
meatballs, 152
melachrinó (to ftohó), 212
melitzánes skórdo stoúmbi, 180
*melitzánes yemistés me maindanó
        kai tyrí*, 179
melitzanosaláta, 93, 94
mint, 62
mousakás tis Soúlas, 154–155
moussaka, Soula's, 154–155
moustárda, 236
moustatsónia, 229
multi-bean soup, 106–107
mushrooms, marinated, 98–99
mussels:
    seafood casserole, 128–129
    with garlic, 130
mýdia me skórdo, 130

New Year's pastry bows, 22
nougat, 237–238
nut and spice rolls with syrup,
        219
nutmeg, 65

octopus:
    baked, 90–91
    pickled, 90
    pie, 167
    ragout, 126–127

olive oil, 67–68, 70–73
olive oil and lemon sauce,
    simple, 82
olives, 67–70, 73–74
okra, 191
oktopodópitta, 167
oregano, 62

pancetta yemistí sto foúrno, 150
pandespáni, 215
paprika, 65
parsley, 62
partridge:
    pilaff, 140
    salmi, 142
    stuffed, 139
pasta, 111
    macaroni with false ragout
        sauce, 115
pásta mílo, 217
pastélli, 228
pastry and sweets:
    almond and tangerine sweet,
        234
    bows, New Year's, 222
    nougat, 237–238
    nut and spice rolls with
        syrup, 219
    peach preserve, 235
    quince delight, 236
    sesame and honey bars, 228
    walnut balls, 229
    see also cake, cookies,
        fritters, pie crusts, pies,
        and tarts

pastitsáda, 146
pastitsáda me kókkora, 133
patátes yiachní, 186
*patátes, glykopatátes kai kydónia
    sto foúrno*, 187
patatoúles tiganités, 95
patatosaláta me piperiés, 110
paté me kimá, 156
paximádia, 21, 64, 203, 204
peach preserve, 235
pear preserve, 233
pérdika piláfi, 140
pérdikes yemistés, 139
petimési, 63
pie:
    cheese, without trousers,
        112
    pumpkin, 218
    walnut, the priest's wife's,
        220
    see also meat pies *and*
        vegetable pies
pie crusts:
    pastry for savory pies, 82
    short crust pastry, 82
pigeons:
    salmi, 141
    with broad beans, 142
pine nuts, 63
pitsoúnia me koukiá, 142
polpéttes, 152–153
polpettóne, 153
polyspória, 106–107
pot roast beef or veal with
    parsley, 148

pork:
  belly, roasted and stuffed,
    150
  Cephalonian meat pie,
    170–171
  Corfiot meat pie, 174
  Ithaca meat pie, 172
  stuffed, 150–151
  Venetian pasticcio, 168–169
  see also ham
potato salad:
  with green peppers, 110
  with lentils, 110
potatoes:
  fried baby, 95
  stewed, 186
  two kinds of baked, and
    quince, 187
poudínga, 207, 208
poudínga apo Kýthera, 209
poudínga inglésiki, 206–207
poultry, 131
  see also chicken; cockerel;
    Cornish game hens;
    partridge; pigeons;
    stuffing, poultry; turkey;
    and woodcock
poutinga, 208
prassópita, 164
prassórizo, 185
preserves. *See* spoonsweets
priest's wife's walnut pie,
  the, 220
psári sto foúrno krassáto, 125
psarósoupa, 102

psitó maindanáto, 148
pudding:
  bread, 207
  caramel, 208
  Elly's orange cream, 210
  English, 206–207
  Kytheran, 209
pumpkin pie, 218

quince delight, 236
quince sauce, 236

rabbit:
  baked, with potatoes, 161
  Cephalonian ragout, 158
  ragout, 157, 160
  with garlic, 159
ragoú apó lagó i kounéli, 160
ragoú me makarónia, 147
ragout:
  Cephalonian, 158
  of beef or veal with
    macaroni, 146–147
  of beef or veal with
    macaroni, Zakynthian,
    147
  of hare, 157
  hare or rabbit, 160
  Swiss chard, 183
  Zante, 145
revithósoupa, 104
rice, 63
rodákino glykó, 235
rolá me sirópi, 219
roló, 153

romaine lettuce and walnut
    salad, 108
rose geranium, 62
rosemary, 62
rovaní, 213
rovaní karýdas, 214
rozedes, 230
rusks, 64
    olive oil, 204
    sweet, 203

salads, 107
    cabbage and arugula, 108
    eggplant, 94
    fennel and orange, 109
    green pepper and potato,
        Koula's, 110
    lentil and potato, 110
    romaine and walnut, 108
    sea urchin, 91
saláta maroúli me karýdia, 108
saláta me finókio kai portokália,
    109
salt cod, 64
    salt cod stew, 120
    salt cod with leeks, 121
sáltsa, 145
sáltsa avgolémono, 84
sáltsa besamél, 83
sáltsa domáta yia makarónia, 81
sáltsa ladolémono, 82
sauces:
    bechamel, 83
    egg-lemon sauce, 84
    garlic, 96

sauces (*cont.*):
    mayonnaise, 83
    simple olive oil and lemon
        sauce, 82
savóro, 118
savoúro, 118
sea urchin salad, 91
seafood. *See* fish
seafood casserole, 128–129
semolina, 65
    fried, 223
sesame and honey bars, 228
sesame seeds, 64
séskala yianchní, 183
sgatzétto, 162
skórda tsigaristá, 98
skordaliá, 56, 96
snacks, favorite, 95
sofríto, 144–145
Soula's eggplant stuffed with
        parsley and cheese, 179
Soula's moussaka, 154–155
Soula's spinach pudding, 187
Soula's squash pie, 164–165
Soula's roast chicken, 132
Soula's zucchini fritters, 194
soup, 101
    bean, Zakynthos, 105
    chick-pea, 104
    egg-lemon soup, 84
    fish, 102
    lentil, 106
    multi-bean, 106–107
    tomato for Lent, 101
    turkey egg-lemon soup, 103

soúpa avgolémono apó galopoúla,
103
soúpa fakí, 106
soupiés me sélino, 128
spanáki sto foúrno, 187
spices, 65
spinach pudding, Soula's, 187
split yellow peas, 42
sponge cake, 215
spoonsweets, 232–233
   almond and tangerine sweet,
     235
   peach preserve, 235
   pear preserve, 233
   quince sauce, 236
   seedless grape preserve, 234
   strawberry preserve, 234
   squash pie, Soula's, 164–165
squid:
   seafood casserole, 128–129
   with rice, 127
stifádo apo lagó, 157
strawberries, wild, 225
strawberry preserve, 234
stuffing, poultry:
   chestnut and sausage, 138
   ground beef and pine nut,
     137
sundried tomatoes, 94
sultanína glykó, 234
sweet potatoes:
   fried, 209
   two kinds of baked potatoes
     and quince, 187
sweet rice cake, 213

Swiss chard ragout, 183
sykomaída, 224
sykópsomo, 224

tangerine cake, 216
taramás, 66
taramosaláta, 42, 47, 88
taramosaláta me avgá réngas, 89
tart, almond, 217
tiganítes, 221
tomato sauce for pasta, 81
tomato soup for Lent, 101
tomatoes, 66
   scrambled eggs with,
     112–113
   stuffed, 188–189
   sundried, 94
tourloú, 190–191
toúrta sokoláta tis Haidós, 211
troúffes apó karýdia, 229
tsigarélli, 182–183
tsigarisména hórta, 184
turkey, 23
   turkey egg-lemon soup, 103
   see also poultry
tyrópita avrákoti, 112

veal:
   Corfiot meat pie, 174
   Lefkada meat pie, 173
   meat and rice croquettes, 155
   meatballs, 152
   pot roast with parsley, 148
   ragout with macaroni,
     146–147

veal (*cont.*):
  ragout with macaroni,
    Zakythian, 147
  with garlic and parsley, 144
vegetable bake, 190–191
vegetable dishes, 175–176
vegetable medley, 192
vegetable pies, 163
  leek pie, 164
  Soula's squash pie, 164–165
  vegetable pie, 166
vegetable stew, green, 184
Venetian pasticcio, 168–169
Venetziániko pastítsio, 21, 40,
    168–169

walnut balls, 229
walnut pie, the priest's wife's,
    220
wine, Ionian, 75–80

yaourtópitta, 216
yellow split pea puree dip, 99
yémisma yia galopóula, 137, 138
yiouvétsi me thalassiná, 128–129
yogurt, 66
yogurt cake, 216

zucchini:
  flowers, fried, 100
  fritters, Koula's, 193
  fritters, Soula's, 194